AMERICAN PHILOSOPHICAL QUARTERLY
MONOGRAPH SERIES

AMERICAN PHILOSOPHICAL
QUARTERLY.

MONOGRAPH SERIES

Edited by NICHOLAS RESCHER

STUDIES
IN
LOGICAL THEORY

Essays by

James W. Cornman

Alan Hausman and
Charles Echelbarger

Robert C. Stalnaker

Montgomery Furth

Jaakko Hintikka

Ted Honderich

Colwyn Williamson

Monograph No. 2   Oxford, 1968

PUBLISHED BY BASIL BLACKWELL
WITH THE COOPERATION OF THE UNIVERSITY OF PITTSBURGH

2,5178

BC
50
S82

PRINTED IN ENGLAND
by C. Tinling & Co. Ltd., Liverpool, London and Prescot

CONTENTS

EDITOR'S PREFACE

This work constitutes the second volume in the Monograph Series which the *American Philosophical Quarterly* inaugurated last year. It is particularly fitting that one of the early volumes in the series should deal with logical theory, since philosophical logic is at present among the most active, fruitful, and diversified areas of research in philosophy. The papers presented here demonstrate the very high standard of current workmanship in this field. The *American Philosophical Quarterly* is most grateful to the learned contributors for authorizing the inclusion of their essays in this collection.

The editor is indebted to Miss Dorothy Henle for her able assistance in seeing the work through the press.

Nicholas Rescher
Pittsburgh
January, 1968

I

Two Types of Denotation

MONTGOMERY FURTH*

IN Frege's philosophy of language, two basic distinctions dominate the treatment of those expressions which, according to his view, are to be sorted as "names." The first distinction divides the *denotation* (*Bedeutung*) of a simple or complex name from its *sense* (*Sinn*). The second distinction, independent of and as it were orthogonal to the first, divides the denotations and the senses of all names into *functions*, described as "unsaturated" or "in need of completion" (*ungesättigt*, *ergänzungsbedürftig*), and *objects*, described as "saturated" and "self-subsistent" (*gesättigt, selbständig*).

Of the four quadrants determined by these two intersecting distinctions, that of "denotations" that are "unsaturated" is not the least problematic, and has attracted increasing attention in recent years;[1] my purpose here is to try to shed some light on it. This is worth doing on two counts. First, although the idea of certain expressions having unsaturated denotation is central among Frege's views and uncompromisingly insisted upon, it never receives a satisfactory explanation in his published writings; further, such explanations as it gets are not merely figurative and obscure, but lead into serious difficulties which Frege appears to have no ready means of resolving. Also the secondary literature that has sprung up around the matter has not so far succeeded in greatly illuminating it.[2] Since Frege's ideas concerning language are nowadays widely (and justly) regarded as highly important, it is of interest to try anew to explain this somewhat vexed aspect of his

* I am greatly indebted to my colleagues Donald Kalish and David Kaplan, to Kalish for very helpful criticism of an earlier version of this paper, and to Kaplan for equally helpful criticism of *two* yet earlier versions. Kalish is not responsible for any remaining shortcomings, although perhaps at this point Kaplan is.

[1] For the most complete survey of Frege-literature to date see the bibliographies to Günther Patzig's two useful collections of some of Frege's essays: *Funktion, Begriff, Bedeutung: fünf logische Studien* (Göttingen, 1962), cited hereafter as "Patzig (1962)," and *Logische Untersuchungen* (Göttingen, 1966), cited hereafter as "Patzig (1966)."

[2] A notable attempt at clearing up some commoner misconceptions is Michae Dummett's paper, "Frege on Functions: A Reply," *The Philosophical Review*, vol. 64 (1955), pp. 96–107, frequently cited below, generally in agreement. But there are divergences, noted where consequential.

theory in a clearer and more manageable form, and to see to what extent the difficulties surrounding it can be dispelled.

There is a second, wider motivation for studying this part of Frege's view, for according to it, expressions with unsaturated denotation include predicate expressions ("concept-words"). As a result, the theory bears directly on an ancient question: Does there exist in the world something that answers to general terms or predicate expressions in a way comparable to the way in which the object *denoted* by a singular term answers to a singular term that denotes it? This, a form of the so-called "ontological problem of universals," goes into Fregean terms as: Have concept-words denotation? And thus his answer, that concept-words *do* have denotation, but *do not* denote *objects*, denoting instead "concepts"—something "unsaturated," "in need of completion," etc.—comes to have more than local interest. I shall not try here to evaluate his view as a contribution to so prodigious a topic as the "ontological problem of universals," confining myself to considering his answer, and the difficulties that surround it, within a Fregean setting; but it is well to bear in mind that the question is an old one, its vitality unimpaired by attempts at its solution within widely varying frameworks other than the present one.

I begin by developing the idea of expressions denoting something unsaturated as it arises in Frege's theory, and then draw attention to the vexing obscurities and difficulties that beset it, ones which Frege himself tries to belittle, but which prove to be serious. In the second section I assemble considerations in favor of a contention which appears to capture the essentials of Frege's idea, but is clearer and more manageable in several ways. In the third and final section this idea, assumed established by the second, is further clarified and consolidated, and in terms of it the difficulties previously encountered are argued to have been dispelled.

I. FREGE ON UNSATURATED DENOTATION

The broad outlines of Frege's theory are too widely familiar to need repeating here; but we should settle from the outset on certain standard ideas and terminology.[3] First, let us use the term "complete name" to describe an expression that either names or purports to

---

[3] Parts of this and the next two paragraphs are borrowed from pp. xiii ff. of my editorial introduction to *The Basic Laws of Arithmetic* (Berkeley and Los Angeles, 1964), the body of which is a translation of portions of Frege's *Grundgesetze der Arithmetik* (Jena, 1893–1903).

name a determinate object. Thus proper names in the ordinary sense are complete names in our sense ("Napoleon Bonaparte," "the Schneekoppe," "Venus" taken as naming a planet), including proper names that do not (as far as we know) name any object but still purport to name some object ("Nessus" taken as naming a centaur, "Nausicaa" taken as naming a young woman, "Venus" taken as naming a goddess). Let us also for the sake of argument admit Arabic numerals as complete names in our sense, such as '9,' thus imagining that the number 9 is a certain determinate object, though an abstract object.

Next, let us take the step—a small one, yet decisive for all that follows—of enriching the category of complete names by distinguishing between *simple* and *complex* complete names, understanding a complex complete name to be a complete name having a complete name as a proper part. Thus "Napoleon Bonaparte" is a simple complete name, but "the elder brother of Napoleon Bonaparte" is a complex complete name which names Joseph Bonaparte. '9' is a simple complete name, but "9^2" is a complex complete name naming the number 81; "3^2" is a complex complete name which, like '9,' names 9. "The shirt of Nessus" is a complex complete name which (as far as we know) does not name anything.

Although, thus enriched, the category of complete names now includes some expressions that might not be counted as proper names in the ordinary sense, nevertheless the concepts of a complete name and of its naming retain a straightforward intuitive content as before. Yet, the step of incorporating complex names into the category is really the key to the entire analysis: for it is to recognize as falling under these concepts, names with a *structure*, names possessing parts which also name (or purport to do so), and which by way of their naming make a contribution to the naming achieved by the whole.

One of the more spectacular consequences of acknowledging complex complete names may be singled out at once. Where we have used the words "is a name of" and "names" to describe a relation between a complete name and a certain object, Frege uses the term "denotes" (*bedeutet*), and speaks of the object named by the name as the denotation (*Bedeutung*) of the name. Then, as the fundamental law of denotation for complex names—as definitive of their semantical structure, governing the contribution of the naming parts to the naming whole—Frege fixes upon the principle that the result of replacing, in a complex name, a constituent name of an object by another name of the same object, necessarily leaves the denotation of the complex name unchanged; thus in "3^2," replace '3' by any other name of 3 (say,

"2+1"), and the result (say, "$(2+1)^2$") is still a name of 9. This principle, the Principle of Interchange[4] for denotation, then invites application elsewhere: for names occur not merely as constituents of other names, but also in *sentences,* and one is inevitably led to ask whether something stands to a sentence with respect to the denotations of the constituent names in that sentence, in the way that the denotation of a complex name stands to that name with respect to the denotations of its constituent denoting names. In other words, one asks whether a Principle of Interchange holds for sentences, such that we may solve for x in:

> "The result of replacing, in a sentence, a constituent name of an object by another name of the same object, necessarily leaves the x of the sentence unchanged";

and Frege obtained the remarkable result that an analogue did hold, and that the solution for x was *truth or falsehood, truth-value.* I shall not repeat his argument here,[5] and henceforth in the paper its conclusion will be assumed as granted. For our purposes, the importance of the conclusion, which in itself merely asserts an analogy, though a remarkable one, is this: It invites us to consider the category of complete names and the category of sentences (as we have distinguished these thus far) as manifesting, in the different guises of naming a certain object and possessing a certain truth-value, a common semantical property. Frege chose to express this by calling the generic property that of "denoting a certain denotation," and he therefore called the truth-value of a sentence its "denotation" and called a sentence a "name" of its truth-value. And I shall follow him in this, thus reflecting the generic property in question by assimilating the category of sentences to that of complete names. But it should be particularly observed that the analogy could be reflected in any number of other ways, and that the reason for choosing this way (besides the desirability of conforming to Frege's terminology where

---

[4] The phrase derives from Carnap, *Meaning and Necessity* (Chicago, 2d ed., 1956), pp. 51 ff. I am not concerned here with the apparent counterinstances to this principle, furnished by such cases as *oratio obliqua,* nor with Frege's ingenious argument to the effect that they are not counterinstances.

[5] See "Uber Sinn und Bedeutung" in *Patzig* (1962), pp. 44–49; cf. also "Function und Begriff" in *Patzig* (1962). Both essays are translated in P. T. Geach and M. Black (eds.), *Translations from the Philosophical Writings of Gottlob Frege* (Oxford, 2d ed., 1960). For more recent versions of Frege's argument, cf. Alonzo Church's review of Carnap's *Introduction to Semantics,* in *The Philosophical Review,* vol. 52 (1943), pp. 298–304, and Church, *Introduction to Mathematical Logic,* vol. I (Princeton, 1956), pp. 24 ff.

possible) is chiefly the resulting compactness and simplicity of theory as well as the opportunity it affords to apply to the case of sentences the intuitions of *complete name* and of *naming* that may be assumed already understood for the earlier, nonsentential cases.[6]

The category of complete names, then, will be taken to include complex complete names, and as a subspecies of the latter, sentences.[7] A denoting sentence, being a sentence with a truth-value, will be said to denote Truth or Falsehood according as it is true or false.

Finally, let us call what is left over when one or more complete names are removed from a complex complete name, an *incomplete expression*, and let us for convenience mark the gap (or gaps) thus left with open parentheses. Accordingly, "the elder brother of ( )," "( )^2," "the shirt of ( )," and so on, will be incomplete expressions. Further, since such sentences as "$3^2=9$," "3 is even," "Napoleon Bonaparte is a man," etc., are complex complete names, "( )$^2=9$," "$3^2=($)," "( ) is even," "( ) is a man," etc., are incomplete expressions.

Thus much for preliminaries. Now we may wonder, in what way should incomplete names be assimilated into the theory of denotation? Frege's answer is unequivocal: An incomplete expression, as we are calling it, is itself to be regarded as a *name*, thus as an expression capable of *denoting a denotation*.[8] But the denotation of a name of this

---

[6] The relation between the analogies established by Frege's argument and the step of actually assimilating sentences to complete names is spelled out somewhat more fully in the editorial introduction to *Basic Laws of Arithmetic, op. cit.,* pp. xx–xxii.

[7] By our explanation of "complex complete name," only sentences containing a complete name as a part will qualify for the title; this restriction answers to the fact that we shall consider the question of "denoting" only for first-order predicates. Cf. n. 30.

[8] Needless confusion has arisen as to whether Frege uses "*bedeuten*" in connection with incomplete expressions to mean *denoting* at all; sometimes it is supposed that he uses it in this case for some undifferentiated notion of "meaning," or again that he uses it in this case for what he calls "sense" in the case of complete names. The idea is unfounded. For "I call *names* only such signs and combinations of signs as are to denote something [*etwas bedeuten sollen*]," *Grundgesetze*, I, p. 32 (=*Basic Laws*, p. 67), italics Frege's; and later, "If from a proper name we remove a proper name that forms a part of it . . . then I call that which we obtain by this means a *name* of a first-level function of one argument," *Grundgesetze*, I, p. 43 (=*Basic Laws*, p. 81), italics Frege's. If *Bedeutung* did not bear its technical sense (in which it is opposed to *Sinn*) for expressions of this kind, it is inconceivable that Frege would have failed to say so here; the same applies to the idiom "name of." For a criticism of the view here rejected, cf. Dummett, *op. cit.,* also his "Note: Frege on Functions," *The Philosophical Review*, vol. 65 (1956), pp. 229–230. (In the quoted passage, as in Frege's writings generally, "proper name" [*Eigenname*] is of course used in the wide meaning that we are expressing by "complete name.")

kind is wholly different in nature; the detonation of a complete name is "saturated," "complete," "self-subsistent," whereas that of an incomplete expression (or incomplete name) is "unsaturated," "incomplete," "unable to stand on its own." The (saturated) denotation of a complete name is an *object*, but the (unsaturated) denotation of an incomplete name is a *function*.

In discussing names up to this point, I have ignored the other aspect of meaning that Frege ascribes to them—that of expressing a *sense*—and I shall continue to do so, confining my attention to "unsaturatedness" at the level of denotation, where we shall find problems quite sufficient to occupy us without proceeding further. Hence, although Frege also describes the sense expressed by an incomplete expression as "unsaturated" and thought of it, like the denotation, as a "function,"[9] I shall use these terms exclusively for denotations that could not stand in the relation *expressed by* to any name. I also adopt for clarity the convention of using the terms "complete" and "incomplete" exclusively to apply to expressions, and "saturated"–"unsaturated" for the denotations of expressions, although Frege uses the two pairs of terms more or less convertibly.[10]

Fregean Metaphors. What then is a function? A complex complete name, as we described it, is formed by completing an incomplete expression by one or more complete names, depending on the number of gaps; suppose for the moment there is only one. Thus, completing "( )^2" by '3' we obtain "3^2," completing "the shirt of ( )" by "Nessus" we obtain "the shirt of Nessus," completing "( ) is even" by '3' we obtain "3 is even," and so on. And Frege describes the *function* that is denoted by the incomplete expression in each case in an analogous way: we are to think of the completion of the incomplete expression, resulting in a complete name, as the syntactical analogue of a "saturation" of the *function*, as if the *function* had a gap; a function is an entity such that, saturated by an object (an argument), it results in an object (the value of the function for the former object as argument). So, just as "3^2" is the result of completing "( )^2" with '3,' so likewise 3^2 (that is, 9) is the result of saturating the unsaturated entity ( )^2 with 3; 9 is "what the function becomes upon being completed."[11] Again, just as "3 is even" is the result of completing "( ) is even" with '3,' likewise 3 is even (that is, the truth-value Falsehood) is the

[9] Cf. Howard Jackson, "Frege on Sense-Functions," *Analysis*, vol. 23 (1962–63), pp. 84–87.

[10] But I shall not alter Frege's terminology in directly quoting him.

[11] Das, wozu sie [=die Function] ergänzt wird, *Grundesetze*, I, p. 36 (=*Basic Laws*, p. 34).

result of saturating the unsaturated entity ( ) is even with 3.[12]

This is indeed strange talk, and there is more. For example, Frege sometimes suggests that the object that is a value of a certain function for a certain argument can be conceived as a whole made of parts fitting together, one part being in this case the unsaturated function, something with a kind of hole in it, and the other the object taken as argument which saturates it, filling up the hole. Though as he immediately goes on to point out,

> To be sure, I have used the word "part" here in a peculiar way. That is, I have transferred the relation between the whole and the parts of the sentence [the type of complete name that happens to be under consideration] to the denotation of the sentence, by calling the denotation of a word part of the denotation of the sentence if the word itself is part of the sentence—an idiom certainly open to attack, because in the case of the denotation, by the whole and one part the other [part] is not determined, and because the word "part" is already used in another sense of bodies.[13]

(These weaknesses in the part-whole metaphor seem eventually to have caused Frege to renounce it entirely.[14])

Again, here is one of Frege's attempts to explain the idea of an entity's being "in need of completion":

> Figurative expressions, used with caution, may after all contribute something towards an elucidation. I compare what is in need of completion [das Ergänzungsbedürftige] with a wrapping, like a coat which cannot stand upright on its own, but to that end requires [bedarf] someone around whom it is wrapped. . . . Here, of course, it should never be forgotten that 'wrapping around'. . . [is] a temporal process, whereas what corresponds to this in the realm of thoughts is timeless.[15]

As the last clause of the above suggests ("realm of thoughts"), the unsaturated entity that Frege is actually contemplating in the passage quoted is a "portion" not of the denotation of a sentence (a truth-value), but rather of its sense (a thought or proposition). This is typical of Frege's later essays, where explanations are in general in terms of sense rather than denotation, and accordingly the

---

[12] I employ Frege's natural practice of *using* a denoting expression to *mention* its denotation. Thus, sentences and incomplete expressions assumed incorporated into the category of denoting expressions, we understand *3 is even is the result of saturating ( ) is even with 3* as equivalent to *the denotation of "3 is even" is the result of saturating the denotation of "( ) is even" with the denotation of "3."*

[13] "Über Sinn und Bedeutung" in *Patzig* (1962), p. 48; in Geach and Black at p. 65. (Here and below I cite English published versions for ease of reference, but translations in this paper are my own.)

[14] Cf. Dummett, "Note: Frege on Functions," also *Grundgesetze*, II, p. 79 (Geach and Black, p. 170).

[15] "Die Verneinung" in *Patzig* (1966), p. 71 (Geach and Black, p. 134).

idea of "unsaturation" that figures in them tends to occur in connection with the possession of sense by an incomplete name rather than the possession of denotation;[16] but the shift is largely one of emphasis and the idea itself, of *Ergänzungsbedürftigkeit*, is similar in the two cases.

A function whose value is always a truth-value Frege calls a *concept* (*Begriff*), and an incomplete name denoting a function of this kind is typically obtained by removing one or more complete names from a *sentence*; thus "( ) is even," used above as an example, is said to denote a concept. Such an expression Frege calls a *concept-word* (*Begriffswort*), and the unsaturatedness of its denotation is sometimes spoken of as the "predicative nature" of the concept.[17] Here is an attempt to explain this species of unsaturation:

> Consider the sentence, "two is a prime number". . . . The first constituent, "two", is a proper name of a certain number, designates an object, a whole, which is not in need of further supplementation [*das keiner Ergänzung mehr bedarf*]. The predicative constituent however, "is a prime number", is in need of supplementation and does not designate an object. I also call the first constituent saturated, the second unsaturated. To this difference among the signs there naturally corresponds a difference in the realm of denotations: to a proper name corresponds an object, to the predicative part, something that I call a concept. This is not supposed to be a definition; for the decomposition into a saturated and an unsaturated part must be regarded as a logically primitive phenomenon which must simply be acknowledged, and is not reducible to anything simpler. I am well aware that expressions like "saturated" and "unsaturated" are figurative and serve only to point towards what is intended: here we must always count upon the reader to understand this and meet us halfway. Nonetheless, perhaps we can make a little more understandable why the parts must be different in kind. An object—e.g., the number 2—cannot logically adhere to another object—e.g., Julius Caesar—without a binding agent [or, cement: *Bindemittel*], and this binding agent cannot be an object but must rather be unsaturated. A logical binding into a whole can only come about by the saturating or completing of an unsaturated part with one or more parts. We have something similar when we complete "the capital of" with "Germany" or "Sweden", or when we complete "one-half of" with "6".[18]

But Frege's best-disposed reader must be prepared to grant that the

[16] Noted by Dummett, "Frege on Functions: A Reply," p. 105 n.; cf. also *Basic Laws of Arithmetic, op. cit.*, p. li.

[17] Cf. "Über Begriff und Gegenstand" in *Patzig* (1962), p. 70 n. 11 (Geach and Black, p. 47 n.).

[18] "Über die Grundlagen der Geometrie, II," *Jahresbericht der deutschen Mathematiker-Vereinigung*, vol. 12 (1903), pp. 368–375, at pp. 371–372. This piece, and its predecessor (*ibid.*, pp. 319–324), are translated together by M. E. Szabo in *The Philosophical Review*, vol. 59 (1960), pp. 3–17. See n. 10.

metaphor of adhesion does not render matters less problematic than does the metaphor of coats, or of part and whole.

Another type of oddity is this: It appears that according to Frege, one may never under any circumstances assert that the denotation of two incomplete names is the *same*, for if "$F(\ )$" and "$G(\ )$" are incomplete names with unsaturated denotation, one is not allowed to write down (even in order to negate it) an identity of the form

$$"F(\ ) = G(\ )"$$

or to entertain the possibility that the denotations of the two names may coincide [*zusammenfallen*].[19]

But possibly the most vexing difficulty of all in connection with incomplete names and their denotations, one that goes beyond the figurative language pervading the explanations of them and such oddities as that just mentioned, is the following. By the talk of name and of denotation, one is led to expect that in this theory there will be for incomplete names something that corresponds to a procedure thoroughly familiar in the case of complete names, that is, the procedure of *specifying what it is that a given name denotes*; but when one asks what form this will take for incomplete names, one finds that several unexpected and puzzling obstacles block the way to an answer. Let me explain.[20]

An Apparent Paradox. If a given category of expressions is regarded as a type of name, denoting something, then there are two procedures that must, so to speak, have meaning or be possible with respect to expressions in that category. One we may call *the ascribing of denotation:* simply saying, of an expression in the category, that it does in fact denote something, is not denotationless. Ideally, we can even imagine this ascription assuming a canonical form, such as (where A is a name belonging to the language in question):

---

[19] Cf. *Grundgesetze*, II, p. 148 (Geach and Black, pp. 180 ff.), and "Function und Begriff" in *Patzig* (1962), at pp. 21 ff. (Geach and Black, p. 26). Remarks in this vein may have helped some readers of Frege to imagine that a function, as here understood, was meant to stand to an incomplete name as its sense, not its denotation. The idea is incorrect, however, stemming from a faulty understanding of the relation between function and course-of-values (*Werthverlauf*); for a discussion of this, cf. *Basic Laws of Arithmetic, op. cit.*, pp. xxxix–xliv. Except for scattered references below, I do not discuss courses-of-values in the present paper.

[20] The way I adopt here of laying out this aspect of the matter does not correspond exactly to anything in Frege's writings, and the terms of art, "ascription (and specification) of denotation," as used below, are mine and not Frege's. But a close consideration of "Über Begriff und Gegenstand," particularly at *Patzig* (1962), pp. 67–70, pp. 76–78 (Geach and Black, pp. 44–47, pp. 53–55), will show that the difficulty is present, and not satisfactorily accounted for. Symptoms of it occur also in "Über die Grundlagen der Geometrie, II," p. 372 n., and in *Grundgesetze*, I, p. 8n. (=*Basic Laws*, p. 37 n.).

B

there exists something that A denotes.

In the case of complete names, this idea is quite straightforward. Let us adopt here and for later use a relation DEN, understood as holding between a name and its denotation, and such that nothing bears this relation to more than one thing (thus ruling out homonymy, and its attendant irrelevant complications). Then the canonical form of ascribing denotation to A might be:

$(\exists x)(A \text{ DEN } x)$.

A second procedure, equally fundamental in connection with names, may be called the *specifying of denotation*: saying, of an expression in this category, what it is that the expression denotes. Canonically, to succeed in specifying the denotation of a complete name A one would have to be justified in asserting something of the form

A DEN a.

Thus, an ascription of denotation to "the Parthenon" assumes the form

$(\exists x)$ ("the Parthenon" DEN x)

and one specification of the denotation of "the Parthenon" would be,

"the Parthenon" DEN the Parthenon,

than all of which nothing could be simpler.

It can (and here, save for this paragraph, it will) go without saying that the notions of ascription and specification of denotation, even as applied within the category of complete names, encompass a vast variety of particular cases and forms; for example, specifying the denotation of "the Parthenon" may, e.g., be accomplished by literally pointing at a certain object and uttering,

"the Parthenon" denotes *that*,

or by use of a definite description that locates the object uniquely, or in various other ways. An additional amplification derives from the assimilation of sentences to complete names, so that, e.g., whatever goes into the specification

"Snow is white" denotes Truth,

will be counted as a specification of denotation for a complete name along with those mentioned above. Furthermore, to determine the correctness of an ascription or a specification of denotation can in particular cases offer severe, even insuperable difficulties. All of these (interesting) matters I ignore, for the immediate point is the contrast which follows.

When we turn to incomplete names, we naturally are prepared by Frege's remarks for something analogous. Perhaps some clue to the form that *ascribing* denotation might take is provided by the metaphors, so that to say of the expression "( )²," for example, that it denoted something would go somewhat like this:

"( )²" *denotes a function, something unsaturated, in need of supplementation, that cannot stand on its own, etc.,*

which suffers from obscurity but might (as Frege suggests) have to be allowed nonetheless, on the grounds that the circumstance it depicted was "logically simple." However, matters become still more questionable when we consider *specifying* denotation for an incomplete name. Suppose, for example, that we are inclined to express this in the form

"( )²" denotes the function *square of*;

Frege's response is to deny flatly that we have achieved our purpose. Why? Because, he says, the expression "the function *square of*" is unsuited to denote a function by the fact that it is *complete*, having no gap or argument-place left open to answer to the essential unsaturatedness of a function. For the same reason, it is illegitimate to attempt to specify the denotation of a concept-word in the manner of, e.g.,

"( ) is a man" denotes the concept *man*,

for the "predicative nature" of a concept precludes its being denoted by an expression like "the concept *man*." It is plain, he says, that the words "the concept *man*" cannot denote a concept, as "( ) is a man" can do, because if we try to form a complex complete name from it and a complete name, the result, e.g.,

"Napoleon the concept *man*,"

is no complex complete name denoting a truth-value, but merely two juxtaposed complete names whose denotations do not "logically adhere" to one another. Or again, by the Principle of Interchange the replacement of a denoting part in a complex name by a name having the same denotation must leave the denotation of the whole unchanged. But if in the complete sentence

"Napoleon is a man"

we attempt to replace the *in*complete portion "( ) is a man" by the words, "the concept *man*," obtaining the result "Napoleon the concept *man*," then not merely does the result have a different denotation from the original: it has none, for it is not itself a complete name at all; and this proves, Frege says, that "the words 'the concept

man' have an essentially different behavior with respect to substitutability from the words 'is a man' in our original sentence; i.e., the
denotations of these two phrases are essentially different."[21]

Because the words "the concept *man*" do not denote a concept, we
seem to be driven into the apparent paradox of saying: the concept
man is not a concept. Likewise, the function *square of* is not a function.
These startling consequences, which at face value would appear to
indicate that something is badly wrong, Frege accepts quite genially:
There is no true paradox here, he says, but "merely a point of language."[22] That is, "there is, I grant, a quite peculiar obstacle in the
way of an understanding with my reader: *viz.*, that by a kind of
necessity of language, my expressions on occasion, taken quite
literally, miss my thought, in that an object is named where a concept
is intended";[23] but the only remedy required is that his reader "meet
him halfway" and "not begrudge a pinch of salt."

But the difficulty goes deeper than Frege is willing to allow, as may
be brought out in this way.[24] The expression employed in specifying
the denotation of an incomplete name, occurring in the context

"$F(\ )$" denotes . . . ,

must itself be a name, and accordingly either a complete name or an
incomplete name. If it is a complete name, then it denotes an object,
and the resulting sentence is false, for we know that the incomplete
name quoted in the specification denotes a concept or other function
(if it denotes anything), and on Frege's principles nothing can be both
function and object. If it is an incomplete name, then the expression
that results is not even a sentence, let alone a true one; for let the
expression employed in the specification of the denotation of "$F(\ )$"
be "$G(\ )$"; then we obtain

"$F(\ )$" denotes $G(\ )$,

the whole of which is not a sentence at all but by Frege's own lights an
incomplete name denoting a concept having Falsehood as value for all
arguments. This way of putting the situation has the advantage that it
avoids the question whether Frege was right in insisting that the

[21] Quoting "Über Begriff und Gegenstand," *Patzig* (1962), p. 73 (Geach and
Black, p. 50), with a change of example (in the original it is "the concept *square
root of four*").
[22] "Über die Grundlagen der Geometrie, II," p. 372 n.
[23] "Über Begriff und Gegenstand," *Patzig* (1962), p. 77 (Geach and Black, p. 54).
[24] Cf. Dummett's review of Geach and Black (1st ed.), *Mind*, vol. 63 (1954),
pp. 102–105, and "Frege on Functions: A Reply," p. 106.

particular phrase "the concept *man*" is in fact a complete name;[25] for the difficulty exists whether it is or not. Either it is, and the previous objections apply, or it is not, and the specification fails for the reason just given. Thus it appears that any attempt at specifying denotation for incomplete names is blocked *in principle* from attaining its intended purpose, and if this is so then it comes into serious question whether we have the right to think of them as expressions that denote, as names, at all.

To this it may be objected: "Frege's argument to the effect that 'the concept *man*' (for example) cannot denote a concept, depends on the assumption that no expression can *denote* a concept unless it is (capable of being) *used as* a predicate in the language containing the expressions whose denotations are in question. But there is no reason to assume this; for denotation is ascribed and specified for these expressions in a metalanguage, which may contain names that do not occur in the object-language,[26] or occur in the object-language but with different meanings. Or the meta-language may be such that its own expressions are subject to different formation-rules from those prevailing in the object-language. So there is no obstacle to saying that in the metalanguage the expression 'the concept *man*' does denote a concept (whatever may be true of it in the object-language), or alternatively saying that the presence of the incomplete expressions '( ) is a man,' or '*G*( )' in a specification of denotation does not preclude the entire affair from being a sentence of the metalanguage capable of truth. That a metalinguistic name of a concept does not *itself* go together with a name of an object to form a complex complete name of a truth-value, or alternatively that the metalinguistic specification of denotation is not a complete sentence by the formation-rules of the object-language, proves nothing: it is even to be expected."[27]

[25] Frege had suggested in *Grundlagen* (pp. 63–64, p. 77 n.), that in everyday language the occurrence of a word with the indefinite article or in the plural without any article was a useful sign that the word was in that occurrence a concept-word, whereas its occurrence with the definite article or with a demonstrative pronoun signified that a determinate object was being designated, hence no concept, and the phrase was a proper name. Much of "Über Begriff und Gegenstand" is devoted to a "vindication" of this "criterion," although in *Grundlagen* Frege had immediately gone on to point out (correctly) that in everyday language it is by no means infallible (p. 64).

[26] Supposing confusion between "object" in (1) "object-language" and in (2) "object, as opposed to function" to be next to impossible, I take no precautions against it.

[27] This point was made by several people with whom I discussed Frege's problem as long ago as 1963, but particularly by Richard Montague and (separately) by David Kaplan. Perhaps its naturalness to our modern eyes partly explains the relative neglect of this portion of Frege's theory even by logicians interested in building upon other portions of it.

This objection has considerable force, and I do not think that Frege meets it in his writings. But it can be met, I think, as follows, and to do so also illuminates Frege's problem. For there is truth in the observation that Frege assumes an expression's denoting a concept to imply its being itself useable as a predicate in the (object-) language, but there is a better reason for this than confusion or mere stubbornness on his part concerning the riches of vocabulary available in the metatheory. The reason is that a purpose of the enterprise itself is precisely to offer an *analysis* or explication of the notion "occurs predicatively," "is used as a predicate"[28] *in terms of* the notion "denotes a concept"; the former is intended to be understood by way of the latter, and the two notions are intended to be related by that strictest of equivalences of meaning which connects explicandum and explicans. In the light of this we can see that for Frege to allow that there could occur genuine cases of an expression's denoting a concept, where yet that expression was *not* capable of occurring predicatively to make up complete sentences, would be for him to risk unravelling the very work that the explication was aimed to do; and thus that his refusal to allow this, however puzzlingly expressed, sprang from an accurate instinct.[29] But if the theory is oriented in the way I suggest, then the difficulties that appear to surround the specifying of denotation for incomplete names should not be explained away in the fashion of the objection, still less shrugged off as Frege wished to do, and it is of interest to trace them to their source.

To sum up this part of our discussion: Frege holds that incomplete expressions are to be regarded as names, having denotation; but his account of what it is that such expressions denote is obscure, resorting to metaphor ("unsaturated") and involving apparent oddities (the apparent impossibility of two such names' denoting the *same* denotation), and even apparent paradox ("the concept *man* is not a concept"). This last seems to be a symptom of something's being badly amiss, for it represents a quite general obstacle to ever specifying the denotation of an incomplete name. There is reason to believe that this difficulty is not simple but quite deep-rooted.

---

[28] On the assumption that the predicative part of a declarative sentence has been agreed to be devoid of "assertoric force," such being ascribed (where it is ascribed) to statements as wholes. Cf. "Die Verneinung," *passim*, and "Über die Grundlagen der Geometrie, II," p. 371.

[29] Since writing the above, I have realized that in "Frege on Functions: A Reply," pp. 106 ff. (a passage I previously did not understand), Dummett may be driving at the same, or at a closely related, idea.

II. Unsaturated Denotation: Whether

The doctrine of unsaturated denotation for incomplete expressions really has two parts. One part is the thesis that an incomplete expression, whatever else may be said about it, cannot *denote an object*, and so that the simple picture of denoting first evoked when we imagined the relation between (say) a proper name in the ordinary sense and the object (person, place or thing) that it names, however generalized, attenuated and made abstract, as it has been by its progressive extensions under pressure of the principle of interchange, culminating in its extension to cover sentences, *cannot* be meaningfully applied to the case of incomplete expressions. The second part is the thesis that nevertheless incomplete expressions can have a property which closely enough resembles the property of denoting for complete names, to justify speaking of the category of incomplete expressions as names also, and saying that incomplete expressions having this property have denotation.

These two theses, being mutually independent, should be discussed separately. To this end, let us formulate Frege's idea as a contention regarding denoting complex complete names, including denoting sentences (=sentences having truth-value), but a contention split into two segments isolable for study: *A denoting complex complete name must contain at least one part which (1) does not denote an object but which nevertheless (2) does have denotation.*[30]

Segment (1). It is, of course, entirely evident that we cannot regard as a final semantical account of a denoting complex complete name, even for the level of denotation alone, a simple enumeration of the denotations of all of its complete parts. For while it is true that a complex complete name is a complete name containing complete parts, and we are taking each complete part to have denotation on its own, an account that stopped here would leave unexplained the most remarkable fact of all: that the complex name is itself a name, denoting a single determinate object, possibly distinct from the denotation of any of its constituents. So we know that a further semantical role is being played within the name, over and above the denoting of their respective denotations by the respective complete parts of the name. It is, of course, this role that Frege endeavours to evoke by images like that of "binding together" the denotations of

---

[30] By our explanation of "complex complete name," the denoting part alluded to will be what Frege calls a "name of a *first*-level function." Later we shall encounter further incomplete expressions, which Frege regards as names of second- and third-level functions—but I do not consider here whether expressions of this kind are to be regarded as names (as *denoting*).

the complete parts into a "whole"; the question is whether an unfigurative description of it is possible.

To see the matter more clearly, let us use as homespun examples of complex complete names, "Plus (3, 2)," "Times (3, 2)," and "Successor (3)," which denote 5, 6, and 4 respectively; and let us for the moment suppose that '3' and '2' ('3' alone, in the last case) exhaust their complete parts. Now, the semantical role that must be played within these names, in addition to the denoting of their respective denotations by the respective complete parts, is twofold: first, that by which the complete parts and the remainder are in each case combined into a whole having a single determinate denotation, and second, that which determines what that denotation is—and it should be noted that it need not be the denotations of the complete parts alone that determine this, for the complete parts of "Plus (3, 2)," and of "Times (3, 2)," as we have distinguished them, are the same, hence (of course) so are the denotations of these parts. But the denotations of the two complex names are distinct. What is it, then, in or of the name, that carries out this function? We have assumed that each of our sample complex names does contain an incomplete expression—"Plus (( )', ( )")," for example, where the accents indicate that the two gaps need not be filled by the same complete name—and so it is natural to look there. In this case, our semantical account of the complex complete name, at this level of meaning, would assign two distinct roles to the expressions making it up: Its complete parts are names denoting certain denotations, and its incomplete part, that which is left over when all of its complete parts are removed,[31] has meaning in a different way; it does not (is not at this stage assumed to) denote anything; it merely *is such that, completed by certain denoting complete parts, the result is a denoting complete name.* We know that such an office is being performed because we know the other ingredients and the result; the current suggestion is that the incomplete part is performing it.

At the beginning of the last paragraph we assumed that for our sample complex names, a residue was indeed left when we removed all of the complete names: that '3' and '2' were the only complete constituents, and this was why it was natural to assign the semantical role in question to the remaining incomplete part. But is the assumption justified in general? The natural response is: of course not, after removal of all of the complete parts, *no* residual expression might

---

[31] In fact, an incomplete part is the residue when *any* of the complete parts are removed, but at the present stage of exposition it simplifies matters to remove them all.

remain. This possibility will at once occur to anyone who thinks of the expression "Plus" above, e.g., as denoting a certain function-in-extension, what Frege calls a course-of-values (*Werthverlauf*), which is an object. This is not the place to enter into the difficult subject of what courses-of-values are, or why Frege holds that they are to be regarded as objects; and fortunately we need not do so, for the possibility can be coped with on other grounds. For grant the possibility that all of the names occurring in the complex name are complete; we *still* know that the semantical role in question is being played, because we still know that the complex name has a single determinate denotation. What is it, then, in or of the name, that carries out this function? Presumably it is here the manner in which the complete parts are composed: the context of their juxtaposition. Yet in principle this does not differ from the earlier cases, the divergence being orthographic: It is a limiting case, differing from (say) "Plus $((\;)', (\;)'')$" in the manner of "$((\;)', (\;)'', (\;)''')$." The semantical role being performed is the same, although wide latitude is possible in the syntactical index by which the playing of that role is signalized.[32]

Because of this, it seems reasonable that we acquiesce in thinking of this index as itself an *expression*, even in the limiting case where—for example, by the use of a functional abstract or course-of-values-name—every part of an acknowledged denoting complete name, in the ordinary sense of "part," is complete. Thus, if it is the manner of composition of these complete parts that has the effect of the resulting compound being itself a complete name, then I wish to think of the empty pattern of composition, the result of replacing every complete name in the complex by empty parentheses (and perhaps accents), as an incomplete expression whose completion issues in the original name, exactly as if the procedure of removing all the complete names had left a remainder, an actual standard sign of (e.g.) functional application, if that is the case we are thinking of.

In thus assimilating the limiting case to the general, seeing the syntactical index of the semantical role of complex-name-forming always as residing in an incomplete expression, we achieve uniformity in our manner of signalizing cases that are semantically alike, and that

[32] Even if removal of all of the complete parts leaves no expression—in the sense of something like "Plus $((\;)', (\;)'')$"—as residue, it remains the case that the denotation of the whole need not be determined by the denotations of the complete parts. For example, completing "$((\;)', (\;)'', (\;)''')$" with "Plus," '3' and '2' in left-to-right order could yield 5 as denotation of the whole, whereas combining the same three expressions in a different manner yielded a denotation other than 5: the Sun, or the null set, or (for all we know at this stage) no denotation at all.

is in principle a good thing; but the direction of assimilation we have chosen is by no means the only one possible.[33] My reason for preferring to see an incomplete expression as carrying out the function in *every* case, is that when we come to the second segment of our contention we shall endeavor to find a parallel between the carrying out of this function on the one hand, and the possession of denotation by complete names on the other. It is much easier to take in the analogies on which this parallel is based if the carrying-out is thought of as done by expressions. At this point, it is enough if we see that the role in question must be carried out for there to be a complex denoting name at all, and that the way of describing this fact which associates the playing of the role in each case with an incomplete expression which is *part* of the complex denoting name, is at least as legitimate as any of various other possible ways, as well as promising future usefulness. We pay a small price for this in having to call (e.g.) "(( )', ( )", ( ) ''')" a *part* of "Plus (3, 2)" (or of "(3, 2, Plus)," as it might better be written if "Plus" is really complete),[34] but it is worth it.

This, then, is what is meant by saying that a denoting complex complete name must contain at least one incomplete part. But, by the foregoing, clearly this part cannot itself denote an object. Some part or parts of it may easily do so,[35] but the whole cannot; better, remove any and every part of it that does so, and a residue remains that does not, even if the residue is the empty schema of composition taken as the limiting case two paragraphs back.

These considerations give us the substance of the first part of our contention: that a denoting complex complete name must contain at least one part that does have semantical significance[36] but does not

[33] For example, in other circumstances one might instead regard the manner of composition of complete names as the paradigm index of the semantical role that is played in complex-name-formation, and take the occurrence of actual incomplete *expressions*, remaining as residue after removal of all the complete names from certain complex names, as a matter of surface grammar—perhaps a practical expedient forced on a language by the fact that it is (at least) technically difficult to devise a different manner of composing names together for *every* relation that one wishes to designate between the denotations of all the complete constituent names and the denotation of the whole. This idea is the well-known basis of the treatment of predicates and relation-words of atomic propositions in Wittgenstein's *Tractatus*.

[34] If "Plus" denotes a course-of-values, the complex complete name could be rendered in *Begriffsschrift* as "$3 \frown (2 \frown \text{Plus})$"; cf. *Grundgesetze*, I, p. 36 (=*Basic Laws*, pp. 94 ff.).

[35] Cf. n. 31.

[36] This merely rules out "parts" like the individual letters of words or the upper halves of parentheses, which also do not denote but which would not normally be assigned the semantical role I have in mind.

denote an object. They do so without invoking the "cement," gaps, coats, and so on of Frege's metaphors, and they avoid the especially treacherous part-whole analogy. It should also be noted that the argument does not depend on any assumption as to *which* part of a complex complete name is incomplete. For all of it, such an expression as

"$3^2 + 2 \cdot 3 + 1$"

could be regarded as e.g.,

the completion of "$(\ )^2 + 2(\ ) + 1$" by "3"
or the completion of "$3^{(\ )} + 2 \cdot 3 + 1$" by "2"
or the completion of "$3^2 + 2 \cdot 3 + (\ )$" by "1"

and so on. This means that so far as the argument is concerned it is not necessary to identify the category of incomplete expressions *in advance* with some variety of expressions already known to us under another title (functional expressions as we ordinarily understand them, or predicative expressions, or the like).

To think of the semantical role in question as carried out by an incomplete expression in every case has another consequence which should be mentioned here. It has been assumed here from the outset that the principle of interchange for denotation (of complete names) is in force, this being of the essence of the notion of a complex name; thus replacement of a complete name in a complex complete name by a name denoting the same leaves the denotation of the whole unaltered. However, it is now open to us to translate this condition into *a property of the incomplete expression* that is the context within which interchange occurs, and to think therefore of languages for which the principle of interchange for denotation obtains, as languages in which incomplete expressions are characterized by this property. For reasons which will become apparent, I wish to elect this manner of speaking. And so henceforward when I speak of the semantical role played by incomplete expressions, this extensionality condition should be understood as incorporated with it: an incomplete expression is such that, not only when completed with certain denoting names the result is a denoting name, but also when successively completed with different names denoting the same, the resulting name always denotes the same. By our assumption on complex names this was the case already; all that is new is its explicit devolvement upon the operation of incomplete expressions.[37]

Segment (2). If an incomplete expression does not denote an object,

---

[37] This passage is referred to in ns. 40, 64.

we should ask ourselves whether there is any reason to say that it denotes at all. For surely Frege's difficulties in explaining what it is for an expression to denote something other than an object are not encouraging; it suggests itself that the idea might better be abandoned altogether, that perhaps such an expression should be regarded as syncategorematic, an "improper symbol" or connective.

On the other hand, we have a powerful motivation to seek a rationale for speaking of *denoting* in connection with expressions of this kind: in the need to introduce quantification in connection with them. The importance of this for Frege is especially plain, since unless predicate and functional expressions are eligible to be replaced with variables bound by quantifiers, such desiderata of his as the explanation of equinumeracy (*Gleichzahligkeit*) and the elegant definition of the ancestral would be impossible—the former requires that we use such an expression as "*there exists* a (first–level) relation such that . . . ," the latter demands something of the form "*y* falls under *every* (first-level) concept such that . . ." And as Frege knew (what Quine more recently has repeatedly urged, though in different terminology), the question whether a term is replaceable with a bindable variable, and the question whether it may be regarded as *denoting* are two sides of one and the same question. One cannot, for example, existentially generalize upon an expression taken as syncategorematic, nor conversely can one refuse to take the position occupied by a genuinely denoting expression, as a position in principle accessible to quantification. To paraphrase a remark of Quine's from a different connection: the principle embodied in the operations of universal instantiation (to a constant) and its quasi-dual, existential generalization (from a constant) is simply the logical content of the idea that the constant in question there denotes.[38]

Frege's need to regard incomplete expressions as open to replacement by variables of quantification—and his need therefore to concede them denotation—comes out also in connection with his interpretation of what nowadays is called the first-order predicate calculus. For to him, this portion of logic is in effect the general theory of (first-level) functions of one or more arguments. The theory that

[38] The paraphrase is of "Notes on Existence and Necessity," *The Journal of Philosophy*, vol. 40 (1943), p. 118; cf. "Reference and Modality" in *From A Logical Point of View* (Cambridge, 2d ed. 1961), p. 146. For Frege's recognition of the point, see *Grundgesetze*, II, p. 255 (= *Basic Laws*, pp. 129 ff.). This motivation for regarding incomplete expressions as denoting is rightly stressed by Dummett; cf. "Frege on Functions: A Reply," p. 99. (But Dummett does not there attempt to reconcile it with the difficulties of their having to denote something other than *objects*.)

collects those properties possessed by *every* singulary function and concept, by *every* binary function and relation, and so on; in his idiom, each theorem of first-order logic asserts that every first-level function (of one or more arguments, as the case may be) "falls within" a certain second-level concept.[39] For this reason such theorems are stated by him using free variables having the totality of first-level functions of one argument (or more, as the case may be) as their range, and there is nothing to prevent these variables from being bound by quantifiers on the one hand, or instantiated to constants on the other, where the constant must then be interpreted as *naming a function* in the range of the original variable.

Nor should it be thought that these considerations merely reflect exigencies prevailing within Frege's particular system, but without wider ramifications: for in ordinary speech, we move unhesitatingly from (e.g.) "Napoleon was a great general and McClellan was not," to "Napoleon was something that McClellan was not," yet as before, our entitlement to do so presupposes that the predicate generalized upon be thought of as naming in some way comparable to that required of singular terms open to the parallel operation. Of course this, like the preceding considerations, is no *argument* for incomplete expressions having denotation; it merely points up further what their lacking denotation entails, and so motivates the search for a rationale of their meaning that would justify regarding them as possessing it.

Heretofore, then, we have been concerned with a conspicuous semantical difference between complete denoting names on the one hand and incomplete expressions on the other; now we seek a similarity: one that may license talk of "denotation" in both cases. Now it is interesting that when Frege actually makes use of the idea of incomplete expressions denoting (as opposed to trying to explain it), the metaphors are dropped and he employs instead a quite clear criterion, namely:

> A name of a first-level function of one argument has a *denotation* (*denotes* something, succeeds in *denoting*) if the proper name that results from this function-name by its argument-places being filled by a proper name always has a denotation if the name substituted has a denotation.[40]

True, this criterion as quoted is laid down for the formalized language of *Grundgesetze* and the possibility of its more general application is

---

[39] For examples and further details, see *Basic Laws*, *op. cit.*, pp. xxxiii–xxxv.

[40] *Grundgesetze*, I, p. 46 (=*Basic Laws*, p. 84). Not mentioned here, but unquestionably part of Frege's notion, is the further condition: that the results of completing such a function-name by distinct complete names denoting the same, are complete names denoting the same. Cf. above text corresponding to n. 37.

not raised at that point. But elsewhere there is in fact much to indicate that Frege thinks of the principle as applicable to any language put forth as suitable for scientific use, and he has no hesitation in chiding (e.g.) predicates of ordinary speech that do not satisfy it as *pro tanto* semantically defective.[41] It appears, then, that in his actual practice Frege takes the condition

> *always results in a denoting complete name upon completion by a denoting complete name*

as the analogue, for incomplete expressions, to the condition

> *denotes an object*

for complete names—in the sense, at least, that incomplete expressions satisfying it are said to "succeed in denoting," and incomplete expressions not satisfying it are called "denotationless." In these terms, the question whether "$(\ )^2$," for example, has denotation, would be viewed not as asking whether there exists an unsaturated entity $(\ )^2$ that "$(\ )^2$" names, but rather as asking whether every completion of "$(\ )^2$" by a denoting complete name of the language is a denoting complete name of the language. The problem is: *is* meeting this condition anything like having denotation?

Following the passage quoted above, Frege remarks that his stipulations of the circumstances under which various types of names in his system "denote something" are not to be taken as *defining* the notion of having denotation, because each of them presupposes that some other type of name is recognized as denoting already. In the present case, for example, it is assumed that we know what denoting is for complete names. Frege himself there actually proceeds to characterize "denoting something" for a *complete* name in terms of meeting the condition that the result of placing it in a denoting *incomplete* name is invariably a denoting (complete or incomplete) name, which manifestly is no definition. As he explains, the purpose of the stipulations is to assure that correctly-formed complex names in the system have denotation if the simple constituent names do, not to attempt to explain in general what denoting is. On the other hand, we have seen that there is difficulty in the idea of incomplete expressions denoting which does not occur in connection with complete names, and so it suggests itself that we take the idea of denoting for complete names as given, and on this basis investigate

---

[41] See *Grundgesetze*, II, pp. 55–56. p. 56 is translated in Geach and Black, p. 159; p. 55 makes it still more explicit that the succeeding strictures are aimed at "piecemeal definition" in natural as much as in constructed languages. Cf. also p. 65.

the *Grundegesetze* criterion for incomplete expressions to find whether meeting it really is a kind of denoting.

So as not to beg any questions, let us adopt a neutral term (i.e., other than "denotes") for incomplete names satisfying Frege's criterion: saying that an incomplete expression "*F*( )" *has the property Z* if for every completion of it by a denoting complete name, the resulting complete name has denotation, and that if this is not so—if completion of "*F*( )" by any denoting complete name does not result in a denoting complete name—then "*F*( )" does not have the property *Z*. Then the problem is: is possessing the property *Z* anything like having denotation?

As we shall see, the answer to this question is: Yes, something like. But it should be observed here that a case can be made for asking that all incomplete expressions of a language should (ideally) have the property *Z*, on grounds of simplicity and naturalness of theory, without prejudging the question whether having *Z* is like denoting. That is, Frege already assumes (as without argument I too shall assume) that the occurrence of a denotationless part in a complex complete name automatically renders the whole denotationless; thus, if a complex complete name does denote, it can be inferred that all of its complete parts denote also.[42] And merely from the explanation of *Z*, if "*F*(*a*)" is a complex complete name and (let us suppose) '*a*' its sole complete part, and '*a*' has denotation but "*F*(*a*)" does not, then obviously "*F*( )" lacks the property *Z*. But a case can be made for asking more than this: namely, for requiring that if a complex complete name does have denotation, then not only do all of its complete parts have denotation but in addition *its incomplete parts have the property Z*—in other words, if an incomplete expression is such as to form a denoting complex complete name on completion by a single denoting complete name, then it forms a denoting complex complete name on completion by any denoting complete name.[43]

For incomplete expressions in Frege's own formal language, this requirement amounts to: function-names that are defined anywhere (=for some object) must be defined everywhere (=for every object), and the argument he typically gives is that if this is not done, "it is impossible to lay down exact laws for them." For concept-words (he argues), the requirement is merely the demand that the Law of Excluded Middle holds for them—and such a demand cannot be withstood; given a concept, each object must be such that either it falls under the concept or does not fall under the concept, *tertium*

[42] This passage is referred to in ns. 48, 53.
[43] This passage is referred to in n. 49.

non datur; the idea of an object's neither-falling-nor-not-falling under a certain concept is incoherent. And having conceded the requirement for concept-words (he continues), we must concede it for function-names in general:

> it is essential that [*e.g.*] "*a*+*b*" always take on a denotation, whatever signs for definite objects may be inserted in place of "*a*" and "*b*". ... [The reason being, that] for every argument *x* for which [*e.g.*] "*x*+1" were denotationless, the function $x+1 = 10$ would likewise have no value, thus no truth-value either, so that the concept
>
> What yields the result 10 when increased by 1
>
> would lack a sharp boundary. The requirement of sharp delimination for concepts thus carries along with it this requirement, of having a value for every argument, for functions in general.[44]

No doubt to our eyes Frege exaggerates in insisting that function-names *must* just on general principles be defined "completely," so that not only the admittedly questionable procedure of "piecemeal definition" is forbidden, but also the giving of conditional definitions —something that could be presented in a more sympathetic light than that with which Frege favors it.[45] On the other hand, he does succeed in bringing out certain advantages in his way of regarding the matter —for example, whether or not it is "impossible" to lay down "exact laws" for function-names on any other basis, it certainly is easiest and most straightforward when they are everywhere defined—in our terminology, when they have the property Z. Furthermore, as he points out,[46] the giving of conditional definitions is itself likely to presuppose that at least certain concept-words have this property— namely, those used in making explicit the area in which the sign being explained is supposed to be undefined; and if this is so it is at least as easy to assign a "don't-care" value to the latter where the former has the value Falsehood, as it is to try to preserve two classes of function-names, some completely defined and the remainder not.[47]

Similar reasoning should mollify those who would see in the con-cession of Z to concept-words in general a contravention of so-called category-distinctions—who would grant, for a crude example, that both "Furth's car is black" and "the Parthenon is black" denote

---

[44] "Function und Begriff" in *Patzig* (1962), p. 29 (Geach and Black, p. 33). The point is elaborately argued in *Grundgesetze*, II, pp. 69–78 (Geach and Black, pp. 159–170).

[45] *Grundgesetze*, II, pp. 77 ff. (Geach and Black, pp. 168–170).

[46] *Ibid.*

[47] For further considerations along this line, cf. W. V. Quine, "Unification of Universes in Set Theory," *The Journal of Symbolic Logic*, vol. 21 (1956), pp. 267–279.

truth-values—Truth and Falsehood respectively—but would balk at conceding Z to "( ) is black" if this meant assigning a truth-value to "the number 4 is black," this on the grounds that numbers are "not the kinds of things" that may meaningfully, truly *or* falsely, be credited with colors. In reply we should first note that the distinction which the category-cartographer has in mind (in some cases, perhaps, a distinction of great importance) can be drawn without appealing to denotationless completions of "( ) is black"; at least, this must be so if the cartographer is to be up to stating the distinction, to which end he must use a concept-word having Z (say, "( ) is a material object"), which then may be employed to separate the false completions of "( ) is black" by names of objects that belong to the intended category from don't-care completions of it by names of objects that do not do so. And secondly, our attitude has the independent advantage, from the category-proponents's viewpoint, of distinguishing two distinct sins which would otherwise be assimilated. For we know that one infallible way of obtaining a denotationless complex name is to complete an incomplete expression with a name that fails to denote.[48] And there is a difference worth reflecting in the grammar, between this sin and the sin of completing an incomplete expression with a name that *does* denote, but whose denotation is on the wrong side of a category-boundary. By not ruling that the resulting complete name in the latter case is flatly denotationless we are enabled to reserve for it a status reflecting its idiosyncrasy, and the punishment may be better fitted to the crime. We need not pursue this issue further here, if it is clear that by asking for the Z condition in the case of concept-words we would not prejudice it.

These considerations suggest that Frege's requirement of Z for incomplete expressions in a scientifically satisfactory language is not so unreasonable as might at first be thought, and that the objections against it which naturally come to mind can be disposed of in other ways. Now let us return to our main question: Does conceding this property to incomplete expressions amount to anything like conceding them denotation?

A clue is provided by our observation above, concerning the link between a term's occupying, within a complex name, a position accessible to variables of quantification, and that term's being regarded as denoting. Let us pursue this for the case of complete names, where we are taking the idea of denoting as understood, and let us introduce here a new type of expression that we may call a (first-order) *virtual*

---

[48] Cf. the above text corresponding to n. 42.

quantifier. Such expressions are incomplete expressions of a kind not hereinbefore encountered: They are such as to yield a complex complete name, not upon completion by a complete name, but upon completion by an incomplete expression. (Because we now have more than one type of incomplete expression, let us call the familiar type— which forms complete names upon completion by complete names —*type* 1, and the new type—which forms complete names upon completion by incomplete expressions of type 1—*type* 2. And because variety among types of incomplete expressions means variety among their gaps, let us adopt Frege's practice of marking the gaps in type-1 incomplete expressions with the lower-case Greek consonants, 'ξ' and 'ζ,' and those in type-2 incomplete expressions with 'ϕ' and 'ψ'; these letters are a mere expository convenience and do not have meaning of any sort.) In particular, the virtual universal quantifier

$$\text{``}[x](\phi(x)),\text{''}$$

forms complex names of truth-values, thus upon completion by a type-1 incomplete expression "$F(\xi)$," the result,

$$\text{``}[x](F(x)),\text{''}$$

denotes Truth if every completion of "$F(\xi)$" by a denoting complete name denotes Truth, and denotes Falsehood if any completion of "$F(\xi)$" by a denoting complete name denotes anything other than Truth. (Hence, we may note, that "$[x](F(x))$" has denotation implies that "$F(\xi)$" has the property Z.)[49]

As is evident from the explanation, the virtual universal quantifier corresponds to a certain portion of the universal quantifier as usually interpreted: that is, it expresses universal quantification with respect to objects *names of which are formable in the language*. Thus, it is that portion of the full universal quantifier in which lies the link between denoting for a name and the accessibility of a position occupied by a genuine name to a variable bound by the full quantifier. Similarly for the virtual existential quantifier, written

$$\text{``}{\sim}[x]({\sim}(\phi(x))),\text{''}\,{}^{50}$$

---

[49] This is obvious if "$[x](F(x))$" denotes Truth; and if it denotes Falsehood then by our assumptions above (refer to text corresponding to n. 43), the fact that the completion of "$F(\xi)$" by some denoting name denotes anything at all entails that "$F(\xi)$" has Z. (The assumption is not that all incomplete expressions are everywhere defined, only that all incomplete expressions that are anywhere defined are everywhere defined.) See also n. 57.

[50] The negation-sign "${\sim}(\xi)$" is a type-1 incomplete expression whose completion by a name denoting Truth results in a name denoting Falsehood, and whose completion by a name denoting any object other than Truth results in a name denoting Truth. Cf. *Grundgesetze*, I, p. 6 (=*Basic Laws*, p. 39).

which upon completion by a type-1 incomplete expression "$F(\xi)$" results in a name,

"$\sim[x](\sim(F(x)))$,"

which denotes Falsehood if every completion of "$F(\xi)$" by a denoting complete name denotes an object other than Truth, and denotes Truth if any completion of "$F(\xi)$" by a denoting complete name denotes Truth. (Hence "$\sim[x](\sim(F(x)))$" 's having denotation implies "$F(\xi)$" 's having Z.)[51]

The effect of a virtual universal (or existential) quantification is then to assert that every object (or some object) nameable in the language has such-and-such a property, and since our present interest is in *names*, whatever additional comprehensiveness may lie in the full quantifier over and above the virtual need not concern us.[52] The essential point is the involvement of *denoting* names in the truth-conditions for expressions formed with our virtual quantifiers. In each case, the denoting of Truth or of Falsehood by the complex expression is explained in terms of the results of completing the type-1 incomplete expression "$F(\xi)$" in question with *denoting* complete names, and the results for denotationless complete names are of no importance. This of course is obvious and to be expected, since the result of completing a type-1 incomplete expression with a non-denoting complete name is a non-denoting complex name;[53] but

---

[51] If "$\sim[x](\sim(F(x)))$" has denotation, then so has "$[x](\sim(F(x)))$," and therefore "$\sim(F(\xi))$" has Z, and therefore "$F(\xi)$" has Z. See n. 49.

[52] Readers of Frege know, of course, that the signs I call incomplete expressions of type 1 and type 2 correspond to what Frege calls "names of first-level functions" and "names of second-level functions" respectively. It is clear that such terminology is not available to us at this point, since the question of ascribing denotation to such expressions is still *sub judice*, and therefore so is the question of calling them "names." But it is also this consideration, as applied to type-1 incomplete expressions, that makes necessary the restriction of the type-2 expression "$[x](\phi(x))$" to the status of *virtual* universal quantifier. For the full universal quantifier "$(x)(\phi(x))$," as usually interpreted, would be explained in Fregean terms by stating that the result "$(x)(F(x))$" of completing it with a concept-word "$F(\xi)$" denoted the True just in case "$F(\xi)$" *denoted a concept under which every object* (no restrictions) *fell*; thus the explanation would presuppose that we already know what a (first-level) "concept" is, and what it is for a concept-word like "$F(\xi)$" to denote such. But we know nothing of the sort; just this is what we are endeavoring to learn. What we have to go on is the capacity of certain expressions to form denoting complete expressions upon completion by denoting complete expressions, and hence the nearest facsimile to quantification over objects that our scheme will support, is quantification with respect to objects that are denoted by some complete expression; only for such objects has such a question as "is the concep word '$F(\xi)$' true or false of it?" a foothold.

[53] Cf. the above text corresponding to n. 42.

as we shall see, a point nevertheless turns upon it. Consider, for example, the result

"$[x](x=x)$"

of completing the type-2 incomplete expression "$[x](\phi(x))$" with the type-1 expression "$(\xi)=(\xi)$." By the explanation given, this denotes Truth, which is as it should be, and the fact that completions "$a=a$" of the type-1 expression by denotationless names "a" (e.g., "Nessus") fail to denote Truth is irrelevant. The intuition is, naturally, that "every (some) object" means, pleonastically, every (some) *existent* object, and no more than this homespun idea is reflected in the feature of the virtual quantifiers to which attention was just called.

Thus we are given that the denotation of a virtual quantification "$\ldots [x] (\ldots F(x))$" depends on the denotation of "$F(a)$" only for *denoting* complete names "a." We now ask: can an analogous idiom be constructed, which (1) stands to type-1 expressions in the way that the (first-order) virtual quantifiers stand to complete names, and (2) is such that having the Z property plays the role for type-1 expressions in this new idiom, that denoting plays for complete names in the one just discussed? This would greatly strengthen the analogy between Z and denotation, for the new idiom would be in effect (though we should not assume this in constructing it) a second-order virtual quantification, involving the Z condition for its instances at just the point where denotation is involved for those of a first-order virtual quantification.

So let us now introduce the expression

"$[f](\mu_\beta(f(\beta))),$"

an incomplete expression of *type 3*, forming complex names of truth-values on completion by incomplete expressions of type 2; the scattered portion "$\mu_\beta \ldots \beta$" marks the gap held open for the latter. In particular, on completion by a type-2 expression "$M_\beta\phi(\beta),$" the result,

"$[f](M_\beta(f(\beta))),$"

denotes Truth if every completion of "$M_\beta\phi(\beta)$" by a type-1 incomplete expression *having the property Z*[54] denotes Truth, and denotes Falsehood if any completion of "$M_\beta\phi(\beta)$" by a type-1 incomplete expression *having the property Z* denotes anything other than Truth.

A second such expression,

"$\sim[f](\sim(\mu_\beta(f(\beta)))),$"

---

[54] The italicized portion will be motivated forthwith.

on completion by a type-2 incomplete expression "$M_\beta\phi(\beta)$," results in a name,

"$\sim[f](\sim(M_\beta(f(\beta))))$,"

which denotes Falsehood if every completion of "$M_\beta\phi(\beta)$" by a type-1 incomplete expression *possessing* Z denotes an object other than Truth, and denotes Truth if any completion of "$M_\beta\phi(\beta)$" by a type-1 incomplete expression *possessing* Z denotes Truth.

In both explanation and typographical design, these type-3 expressions resemble the first-order virtual quantifiers: They are an idiom standing to type-1 incomplete expressions much as the type-2 virtual quantification already introduced stands to complete names. But note that the resemblance does not rest on assuming that type-1 expressions *denote* (as denoting complete names are required for the explanations on the first-order level); instead, what figures at the corresponding point in the truth-conditions is their possessing Z. And by the same token, we are not yet ready to call these new, second-order expressions themselves virtual *quantifiers*. To do so would automatically commit us to the attitude toward type-1 constants whose justifiability we are considering.[55]

To see better the involvement of the Z condition in these cases, let us consider the completion of "$[f](\mu_\beta(f(\beta)))$" by a specific type-2 incomplete expression: for example, by

"$[x]((\phi(x)) \rightarrow (\phi(x)))$,"[56]

where the result of completing the type-3 expression is then

"$[f]([x]((f(x)) \rightarrow (f(x))))$."

By the explanation of "$[f](\mu_\beta(f(\beta)))$," the name just mentioned denotes Truth if every completion of "$[x]((\phi(x)) \rightarrow (\phi(x)))$" by a type-1 incomplete expression *possessing* Z denotes Truth. But here the reason is manifest why the stipulation is confined to type-1 expressions having Z: for let "$F(\xi)$" be a type-1 expression not having Z, then the completion by it of "$[x]((\phi(x)) \rightarrow (\phi(x)))$"—namely, "$[x]((F(x)) \rightarrow (F(x)))$"—does not denote Truth, or anything else, because not every completion of "$(F(\xi)) \rightarrow (F(\xi))$" by a denoting

---

[55] Cf. n. 38, and the second half of the paragraph it annotates.

[56] The conditional-sign "$(\xi) \rightarrow (\zeta)$" is a doubly-incomplete type-1 incomplete expression; completed by a name denoting Truth in the ξ-place and a name denoting any object other than Truth in the ζ-place the result is a name of Falsehood; completed by (complete) denoting names of any other kind in the ξ- and the ζ-place the result is a name of Truth. Cf. *Grundgesetze*, I, p. 12 (=*Basic Laws*, p. 51).

complete name denotes Truth.[57] Accordingly, if type-1 expressions not having Z were allowed to count in our explanation of "$[f](\mu_\beta(f(\beta)))$,"[58] the result would be—most anomalously—that

$$\text{"}[f]([x]((f(x)) \rightarrow (f(x))))\text{"}$$

did not denote Truth, and was in fact denotationless.

Thus the position does resemble that which we reached for the first-order virtual quantifier "$[x](\phi(x))$." There we saw that the reason for explaining the denotation of "$[x](F(x))$" in terms of the completion of "$F(\xi)$" by *denoting* complete names, was essentially that otherwise names such as "$[x](x=x)$," which obviously ought to denote Truth, would not do so, nor denote anything. Similarly here: if we did not explain the denotation of "$[f](M_\beta(f(\beta)))$" solely in terms of the completion of "$M_\beta\phi(\beta)$" by type-1 expressions *having* Z, then names like "$[f]([x]((f(x)) \rightarrow (f(x))))$," which obviously ought to denote Truth, would not do so, nor denote anything. And so the requirement of Z, occurring where it does in the explanation of the type-3 incomplete expression "$[f](\mu_\beta(f(\beta)))$," is analogous to the requirement of denotation, occurring where it does in the explanation of the type-2 incomplete expression "$[x](\phi(x))$."[59]

Similar remarks apply to the virtual existential quantifier "$\sim[x](\sim(\phi(x)))$" and the type-3 expression "$\sim[f](\sim(\mu_\beta(f(\beta))))$." By the explanation of the former, if a complete name "$F(a)$" denotes Truth, it follows that "$\sim[x](\sim(F(x)))$" denotes Truth also;[60] this is existential generalization with respect to objects in the scheme of virtual quantification. In formal mode, it registers that completion of "$F(\xi)$" by some complete name results in a complex name denoting Truth—and we know that for this to come about the completing name must denote. By the explanation of "$\sim[f](\sim(\mu_\beta(f(\beta))))$," if a complete name "$M_\beta(F(\beta))$" denotes Truth, it follows that "$\sim[f](\sim(M_\beta(f(\beta))))$" denotes Truth also; this is the parallel, for type-1 incomplete expressions, to the transition of existential generalization with respect

---

[57] The completions where "$F(\xi)$" is undefined. See the explanation of "$[x](\phi(x))$," text corresponding to n. 49.

[58] So that the italicized portions were omitted, cf. n. 54.

[59] Lest our example be thought tendentious (since, in less cautious language than hitherto, "$[x]((F(x)) \rightarrow (F(x)))$" denotes the truth-value thereof that *for every object, either it does not fall under F or it does*, which is simply the material-mode reflection of the formal-mode statement that the predicate "F" has the property Z), it should be noted that other examples would do as well. For instance,
$$\text{"}[f]([x]([y]((x=y) \rightarrow (f(x)=f(y)))))\text{"}$$
denotes Truth, therefore if
$$\text{"}[x]([y]((x=y) \rightarrow (F(x)=F(y))))\text{"}$$
fails to denote Truth, then "$F(\xi)$" must lack the property Z.

[60] Cf. the above text corresponding to ns. 50–51.

to names of objects. In formal mode, it registers that completion of "$M_\beta\phi(\beta)$" by some incomplete expression results in a complex name denoting Truth—and we know that for this to come about the incomplete expression must have the property Z.[61] Thus the parallel holds on this side also.

Now let us bring these considerations to bear on cases closer to home. Consider the complex complete name (assumed to denote Truth)

"Socrates is wise,"

or, as we may rewrite it for (nothing but) easier handling,

"wise (Socrates)."

From the foregoing, this may be regarded in either of two ways: either as the result of completing "wise (ξ)" (a type-1 incomplete expression) with "Socrates" (a complete name), or as the result of completing "ϕ(Socrates)" (a type-2 incomplete expression) with "wise (ξ)" (a type-1 incomplete expression). If it is thought of in the former way, then it is the fact that "Socrates" has denotation that legitimizes the transition of (virtual) existential generalization on it,

from "wise (Socrates)" to "$\sim[x](\sim(\text{wise }(x)))$";

if it is thought of in the latter way, it is the fact that "wise (ξ)" has Z legitimizes an analogous transformation on it,

from "wise (Socrates)" to "$\sim[f](\sim(f(\text{Socrates})))$."

With this parallel before us, the possibility of reading the type-3 expressions in question as a variety of virtual quantifiers is naturally greatly reinforced. And so two suggestions are in order. (1) Just as "$\sim[x](\sim(\text{wise }(x)))$" may be rendered as (the truth-value) *there is something which is wise*, so also "$\sim[f](\sim(f(\text{Socrates})))$" may be rendered as (the truth-value) *there is something which Socrates is*.[62] (2) Just as "$[x](F(x))$"—for example, "$[x](x=x)$"—is a universal virtual quantification entailing that any formable instance "$F(a)$" (let one such be "$F(\text{Socrates})$," i.e., "Socrates$=$Socrates") denotes Truth provided only that "a" ("Socrates") has denotation, so also "$[f](M_\beta(f(\beta)))$"—for example, "$[f]([x]((f(x)) \rightarrow (f(x))))$"—is a virtual quantification as well, entailing that any formable instance "$M_\beta(F(\beta))$" (let one such be "$M_\beta(\text{wise}(\beta))$," i.e., "$[x]((\text{wise}(x)) \rightarrow (\text{wise}(x)))$") denotes Truth provided only that "$F(\xi)$" ("wise (ξ)") has the property Z.

---

[61] Cf. ns. 49, 51 above, for the cases where "$M_\beta\phi(\beta)$" is "$[x](\phi(x))$" and "$\sim[x](\sim(\phi(x)))$" respectively; reasons of the kind given there apply generally.
[62] Cf. below, Sect. III, for the manner of ontological commitment involved.

Of a piece with these moves, less a separate suggestion than an alternative form of those already made, is to take *satisfaction of the Z condition by a type-1 incomplete expression as a kind of denoting*. For as has been pointed out,[63] if an expression within a complex name of a truth-value is regarded as occupying a position accessible to variables of quantification, then none but terminological reasons militate against regarding that expression as denoting. Thus, it is suggested, *just as, if a complete name denotes an object, it is said to have denotation, so also, if a type-1 incomplete expression has the property Z, then it too may be said to have denotation.* This is the second segment of the contention we are considering.[64]

By the first segment, we know that "having denotation" in connection with type-1 incomplete expressions cannot mean, *denoting an object.* Hence the two segments taken together suggest that there are two types of denotation, one for complete, the other for incomplete names.[65] I shall accept this suggestion also, and mark the difference between the two types by saying that complete names have *saturated denotation*, and that incomplete names have *unsaturated denotation*. But it must be carefully borne in mind that for an incomplete expression to have unsaturated denotation, as here explained, *is not for it to bear the denoting relation appropriate to complete names* (i.e., DEN) *to an "unsaturated entity"*; it is for it to have Z. The point is stressed because the contention can so easily be misinterpreted by someone holding firmly to a single type of denoting—the relation in which "Napoleon" stands to Napoleon—as asserting that complete names bear this relation to saturated entities, and that incomplete names bear this relation to unsaturated entities. We are then faced with the question what the latter may be, and the difficulties of "Über Begriff und Gegenstand" are the unwelcome result. But the proposal resulting from our study of the contention is different from this. It consists in regarding the matter not in terms of two types of denoted "entities," but in terms of *two types of denoting*, extending the differentiation back into the denoting relation itself. On this basis, an incomplete name's meeting the Z condition is not a *sign* that it therefore denotes (in the manner of a complete name) something mysterious (unsaturated): it is itself a second manner of denoting.

---

[63] N. 38, and the second half of the paragraph it annotates.

[64] It should not be forgotten that we are continuing to associate with type-1 incomplete expressions the extensionality condition singled out in text corresponding to n. 37 and also in n. 40. Cf. Sect. III below.

[65] As I shall begin calling them, cf. n. 52.

III. Unsaturated Denotation: What. Two Types of Denotation

In Sect. I, we called attention to the two procedures of *ascribing* and *specifying* denotation for names; in the case of complete names, we imagined this as assuming a simple canonical form of

(i) $(\exists x)(A \text{ DEN } x)$

for ascription of denotation to a name A, and

(ii) $A \text{ DEN } a$

for specifying A's denotation. It was upon attempting to apply these ideas to incomplete expressions that we struck a serious obstacle, viz., that on Frege's account of the matter, it apparently was impossible to specify the denotation of an incomplete expression; one either mentioned an *object*, or else did not succeed in making a complete statement. Ascription of denotation to these expressions was accordingly problematic also.

One reaction to this would have been to conclude that Frege's idea of unsaturated denotation must simply be abandoned: Either (1) that we should cease to speak in his way of "functions" and "concepts," and should instead regard the so-called incomplete expressions as denoting (i.e., as standing in DEN to) certain *objects* such as classes or courses-of-values, or else (2) that we should drop the idea of denotation in connection with these expressions entirely. But we saw that this reaction would be premature, for as against (1) there is reason to believe that some portion of a complex complete name *cannot* denote an object, and as against (2) we found cause to regard this part as possessing properties displaying some remarkable similarities to denoting.

These considerations suggest that the real cause of the difficulty lies in attempting to render the ideas of ascribing and specifying denotation for incomplete names directly in terms of DEN, e.g., in looking for an appropriate completion of

"$F(\xi)$" DEN . . . ,

whereas we now can see what variant form these ideas must take for names of this kind. If an incomplete name's denoting is its having the property Z, then a first approximation to ascribing denotation to such a (singly-incomplete) name B would be ('a' a syntactical variable over complete names):

for every a, if $(\exists x)(a \text{ DEN } x)$, then $(\exists y)((\text{the completion of } B \text{ by } a)$ DEN $y)$.

For short,

$(a)((\exists x)(a \text{ DEN } x) \rightarrow (\exists y)(C(B, a) \text{ DEN } y)).$[66]

Or, equivalently,

$(a)(x)(a \text{ DEN } x \rightarrow (\exists y)(C(B, a) \text{ DEN } y)).$

Yet, we can be more explicit still for we can articulate the principle, to which attention has already been called, that an incomplete expression is such that successive completions of it by names denoting the same are names denoting the same. This should now be incorporated into the account of such expressions denoting, since it is the property by virtue of which a complex complete name not only has a denotation, but has a denotation that is a function of the denotations (and nothing further than the denotations) of its complete parts. And so the full ascription is:

(iii) $(a)(\beta)(x)(a \text{ DEN } x$ and $\beta \text{ DEN } x \rightarrow (\exists y)(C(B, a)$
DEN y and $C(B, \beta) \text{ DEN } y)).$

Thus, if B satisfies (iii), B denotes. But we cannot express this circumstance, parallel to (i), by writing something of the form

$(\exists f)(B \text{ DEN } f).$

For if we could, we should then be faced with the problem how to construe *specifying* the denotation of B conformably with (ii); our alternatives would be to use the form

$B \text{ DEN } F(\xi),$

or the form

$B \text{ DEN } a,$

and we should be no better off than at the outset.

The parallel to (i) is, rather, this:

(iv) $(\exists f)(a)(x)(a \text{ DEN } x \rightarrow C(B, a) \text{ DEN } f(x)),$

where the idiom "$(\exists f)(\ldots f(\ ) \ldots)$" of the metalanguage is to be understood as a virtual quantifier similar to "$\sim[f](\sim(\mu_\beta(f(\beta))))$" of the language under study. Thus the ascription (iv) results from completion of this quantifier by the type-2 expression

$(a)(x)(a \text{ DEN } x \rightarrow C(B, a) \text{ DEN } \phi(x)),$

and to specify the denotation of B is accordingly to provide in the ϕ-place of this expression a name "$F(\xi)$" of what it is that B denotes:

(v) $(a)(x)(a \text{ DEN } x \rightarrow C(B, a) \text{ DEN } F(x)).$

---

[66] The abbreviation "$C(a, \beta)$" for "the completion of a by β" could be complicated to extend to completions of incomplete names having arbitrarily many gaps. I shall deal henceforth only with singly-incomplete names.

Here some examples will be helpful. An example of an ascription of denotation to "Napoleon" is, in our canonical form,

$(\exists x)(\text{"Napoleon" DEN } x)$,

a sample specification of what this name denotes is,

"Napoleon" DEN Napoleon.

An example of an ascription of denotation to "(ξ) is a man" is, in our canonical form,

$(\exists f)(a)(x)(a \text{ DEN } x \rightarrow C(\text{"}(\xi) \text{ is a man," } a)$
DEN the truth-value thereof that $f(x)$),

and a sample specification of what this name denotes is,

$(a)(x)(a \text{ DEN } x \rightarrow C(\text{"}(\xi) \text{ is a man," } a)$
DEN the truth-value thereof that x is a man).

To apply this to an incomplete name that is not a concept-word, consider "$(\xi)^2$." I ascribe it denotation, thus:

$(\exists f)(a)(x)(a \text{ DEN } x \rightarrow C(\text{"}(\xi)^2\text{," } a) \text{ DEN } f(x))$;

I specify its denotation, e.g., thus:

$(a)(x)(a \text{ DEN } x \rightarrow C(\text{"}(\xi)^2\text{," } a) \text{ DEN } x \cdot x)$.

Let us boil this down still further. The specification of denotation for "Napoleon" asserts that this name and a specified object, in that order, stand in the relation DEN; that is, it attributes to the name the property of standing in DEN to the object. The property attributed by the specification of denotation for "(ξ) is a man," on the other hand, is more complicated: It is the property of being such that upon completion by any denoting complete name the result denotes the truth-value thereof that the completing name's denotation is a man.[67]

These are the two types of denotation. One holds between denoting complete names and the world (the "realm of denotations") in the most straightforward possible way; it is depicted in the metalanguage by the simple, doubly-incomplete type-1 expression,

ξ DEN ζ.

If all complete names were simple, this would be the only type of denotation. But if complete names are to be complex, a second type of denotation must be in effect also; it too holds between expressions (incomplete, in this case) and the world, but in the much more complicated way depicted in the metalanguage by the doubly-incomplete expression of mixed type,

---

[67] This of course is not circular, no more than to describe the property attributed to the complete name "Napoleon" as that of denoting Napoleon.

$(a)(x)(a \text{ DEN } x \rightarrow C(\xi, a) \text{ DEN } \phi(x)).$

Both types of denotation can be ascribed to names, and—for both types of denotation—what it is that names denote can be specified. But the ascriptions and specifications take distinct forms—(i) and (ii) for complete names, (iv) and (v) for incomplete names—which are inherited from the distinct ways in which "the denoting expressions and the world" hang together in the two cases.

In the light of the foregoing, we can see quite clearly the cause of the metaphors and lame analogies to which Frege was driven in trying to explain the idea of unsaturated denotation, as well as the seeming paradox involved in "the concept *man*" not denoting a concept. For all of these are the characteristic expression of a person's attempting to force the second type of denotation into the mold of the first: seeing very clearly that incomplete expressions must be operative, have some fashion of meaning, at the level of denotation, must denote in some way, and seeing simultaneously that their denotation could not be simply an (another) *object*, both of these undoubtedly for the kind of reason spelled out in the first segment of our contention, his response was to try to adapt the idiom

$A \text{ DEN } a$

in various more or less distorted ways; he admitted that none of them succeeded in bringing out what he had in mind, but (I conjecture) he feared that to give them up would be to surrender denotation for incomplete expressions altogether. To what degree he was "held captive by the picture" that renders all denoting as of the first type, one can no more than guess; but the evidence suggests to me that he never was able to locate it accurately and shake it off.

The same considerations explain the oddity noted in Sect. I, that apparently according to Frege no two incomplete expressions can have the *same* denotation: in material mode, that "identity cannot hold between concepts."[68] For in terms of the two types of denotation, if two complete names "have the same denotation," the situation may be described thus:

    there exists an object that both A and B denote,

or

    $(\exists x)(A \text{ DEN } x \text{ and } B \text{ DEN } x);$

but if two incomplete names Γ and Δ (let them be concept-words) "have the same denotation," the situation is this:

[68] Cf. n. 19.

the completions of Γ and Δ by complete names denoting the same object [=argument] are always complete names denoting the same object [=value],

or

$$(\exists f)(\alpha)(\beta)(x)(\alpha \text{ DEN } x \text{ and } \beta \text{ DEN } x \rightarrow$$
$$C(\Gamma, \alpha) \text{ DEN } f(x) \text{ and } C(\Delta, \beta) \text{ DEN } f(x)).$$

And as the former circumstance stands to the relation

$$\xi = \zeta,$$

the latter stands to the relation

$$[x](\phi(x) = \psi(x)).[69]$$

The treatment of denotation suggested here, then, resolves a number of difficulties in Frege's formulations. The *metaphors* are dispensed with. (Of course, they retain some heuristic value; but one is not reduced to the plea that *only* metaphor is possible, that one can only "hint.") The *oddities*, like its being illicit to assert that the denotation of two incomplete expressions is the same, are dispelled. And the apparent consequence of the difficulty about "the concept *man*"—that one could not specify the denotation of the incomplete name "(ξ) is a man"—is avoided by the manner of specification we have given. Of the last problem, Dummett[70] has written that "this (at first sight trivial) difficulty shows conclusively that the two parts of Frege's theory—the method of classifying expressions into 'proper names,' first- and second-level concept-words, etc., and the doctrine that each of these kinds of expression stands for [=denotes] something—will not hang together; some modification is called for." It is hoped that the formulation in terms of two types of denotation accomplishes the hanging-together for at least a version of Frege's theory. The reader may judge for himself the extent of "modification" involved.

University of California, Los Angeles

[69] Cf. *Basic Laws*, *op. cit.*, pp. xlii–xliv.
[70] "Frege on Functions: A Reply," p. 107.

II

Language-Games for Quantifiers

JAAKKO HINTIKKA

Logical Expressions. One way of looking at logic is to view it as a study of certain words and phrases which we may label *logical expressions.* Whether or not one can thus obtain a general definition of the province of logic, this point of view is useful for many purposes.[1] For instance, quantification theory may be characterized from this point of view as the study of the phrases "there is," and "for every" over and above the study of the words "not," "and," and "or," which are already studied in propositional logic, plus whatever terms are required to express predication. I shall call these phrases and other expressions with similar meanings *quantifying expressions.*[2]

In books and papers on logic, some aspects of the behavior of these expressions are studied. However, they are usually studied mainly as they appear in more or less strictly regimented systems of formal logic. The meaning they have in unregimented discourse is not often discussed directly, nor is the relevance of these formal studies to the more ordinary uses of the quantifying expressions "there is," and "for every." In this paper I shall deal with these questions, questions on whose importance I scarcely need to enlarge.

---

[1] On the subject of logical vocabulary, see P. F. Strawson, *Introduction to Logical Theory* (London, 1952), pp. 47–49, 57; W. V. O. Quine, "Mr. Strawson on Logical Theory," *Mind*, vol. 62 (1953), pp. 433–451, especially p. 437.

[2] In this paper, only those quantifying expressions are studied which are roughly synonymous with the usual existential and universal quantifiers. Non-standard quantifiers, such as "at least two," "at most three," "many," "most," etc. are illuminated only in so far as they behave in the same way as standard quantifiers or are definable in terms of these. Furthermore, all differences between the different ordinary-language equivalents to standard quantifiers are disregarded, although some of them are of considerable interest. In particular, I shall disregard the close relation which there is between some of these idioms (e.g., "some," "all," etc.) and the "quantitative" relation of a whole to a part. Interesting as this relationship is in many respects, not just as a reason for some of the differences between different quantifying expressions, it is in my view less important than the problem of interpreting quantifying expressions when they are conceived of in the usual terms of "ranging over" a domain of discrete individuals. Of the quantifying expressions of ordinary language, "there is" (or "exists"), and "for every" perhaps come closest to this type of quantifying expression and are therefore considered here in the first place.

Meaning as Use. Plenty of advice is in fact available to tell me how to straighten the defect just mentioned. Much of this advice is summed up in the famous remark of Wittgenstein's: "The meaning of a word is its use in the language."[3] This dictum is not unequivocal, however, not even if we recall that it was only supposed by Wittgenstein to cover a large class of words, not the meanings of all possible words that there are. Here I am not interested in bringing out all the different aspects of Wittgenstein's advice. For my present purposes it suffices to confine our attention to one of the most important things Wittgenstein apparently meant by his dictum. This aspect of his remark has not always been brought out as clearly as it ought to have been.

It is perhaps easier to say what in Wittgenstein's *dictum* I am *not* interested in (for the purposes of this paper). Sometimes distinction is made between the use of words and the use of language.[4] Under the former title philosophers have considered the use of words for the purpose of forming sentences or for referring. Under the latter title, they have usually considered the different language acts or speech acts which one can perform by uttering or by writing a sentence. The uses of language are then those uses which one can make by uttering or writing something.

It seems to me that this distinction is not an exhaustive one, and that the uses of words which I am primarily interested in here are largely forgotten if the situation is described in these terms. It is obvious that Wittgenstein did not have in mind only the uses of words for the purpose of constructing sentences out of them when he coined his slogan. Furthermore, he certainly did not have in mind only the acts one can perform by saying something or in saying something. It is not for nothing that Wittgenstein often speaks of the uses of *Wörter*, that is to say, of individual words, and not only of the uses of *Worte*, that is to say, of words articulated into sentences.[5] The study of the different types of speech-acts does not exhaust the import of Wittgenstein's advice. The uses we are invited to consider do not always take the form of locutionary or illocutionary acts. Wittgenstein is not asking what we do or can do by uttering a sentence. He is also asking what we must be able to do or what people must generally do in order

---

[3] Ludwig Wittgenstein, *Philosophische Untersuchungen—Philosophical Investigations* (Oxford, 1953), Pt. I, sect. 43: "For a *large* class of cases—though not for all—in which we employ the word 'meaning' it can be defined thus: the meaning of a word is its use in the language."

[4] Cf. e.g., Gilbert Ryle, "Ordinary Language," *The Philosophical Review*, vol. 62 1953), pp. 167–186.

[5] *Philosophical Investigations*, Pt. I, sects. 6, 9, 10, and 11.

for us to understand a word.[6] He is calling our attention to a certain environment of types of action or activities which a word often has and outside which it loses its meaning (or its use, if you prefer).

These activities may be activities one performs by uttering a sentence, but they need not be. The verb "thank" loses its use (or meaning) in the absence of the custom of thanking. This custom happens to be such that one can thank by saying "thank you." However, the fact that one can do this is largely inessential to the connection which there is between the custom (or institution) of thanking and the meaning of the verb "to thank." For we could use this verb meaningfully even if it were not our custom to thank by saying anything but (for instance) merely by means of certain gestures. As our actual customs go, it is certainly possible to thank someone without using the verb "to thank." In the case of certain other words, for instance, of the verb "to score" (in a game), the activities we must be able to master, if only from the point of view of a spectator, are such that they are never performed merely by saying something. Thus, for one who is primarily interested in the activities which constitute the natural environment of a word and from which it gets its meaning, the things one can do by means of words are not of a central importance. What is important is the connection between words and the activities which typically surround it. The aspect of Wittgenstein's advice which I want to take up here is therefore closely related to his notion of a language-game. "I shall also call the whole, consisting of language and the activities into which it is woven, the 'language-game' "; "Here the term language-game is meant to bring into prominence the fact that the speaking of language is part of an activity, or a form of life."[7] The emphasis is here as much and more on the actions in the framework of which the use of words occurs as on the actions which one can perform by using certain words. The activities which typically surround a word and from which it gets its meaning might be called the language-game in which the word in question is at home.

Relation to Operationalism. An extreme, and exaggerated, form of this dependence of certain words on non-linguistic activities for their meaning is claimed to obtain by the group of doctrines known as

---

[6] Ryle, *op. cit.*, warns us not to mistake *use* (in speaking of the use of language) to mean *utilization*. But surely Wittgenstein constantly assimilates these ideas to each other. His favorite term *Gebrauch* is ambiguous in the same way as the English word *use*, and could often be taken in the sense of usage; but on other occasions the presence of the ideas of application and utilization are unmistakable. These ideas are often still more obvious when Wittgenstein uses words like *Verwendung* or *Anwendung*, which he also frequently does. (See *Philosophical Investigations*, Pt. I, sects. 11, 20, 21, 23, 41, 42, 54, 68, and 84.)

[7] *Philosophical Investigations*, Pt. I, sects. 7 and 23.

operationalism.[8] In spite of the vagueness and crudity of operationalistic doctrines some aspects of these views merit a comparison with those aspects of Wittgenstein's ideas we are interested in here. It is important to realize, however, that the interpretation I am putting on Wittgenstein's words does not commit me to anything like operationalism. On a typical operationalistic view, to make a statement containing operationally defined words is to make a prediction, as it were, concerning the outcome of the operations which are associated with these words. What is more, it is normally required that these operations can be performed once and for all. It is required, moreover, that they can be performed in only one way. It is also required that to each operationally defined word there is but one defining activity or "operation" associated with it.

These three requirements (together with other similar requirements which strict operationalism imposes on the activities from which our words receive their meaning) seem to me exceedingly narrow-minded. There does not seem to be any reason to deny that a word may be connected with an activity or mode of action which does not necessarily terminate or whose termination point is at least unpredictable. There also seems to be no reason whatsoever to deny that the activities in question can be performed in many alternative ways. Furthermore, one has to realize that a word may be connected with reality not through a single operation, but rather through a network of subtle interrelations which involve a good many theoretical assumptions.

In spite of all these shortcomings, there are some purposes which an operationalistic view of language may serve. It serves to bring out, albeit in a distorted form, one aspect of the notion of "the use of language" which is sometimes forgotten. If its exaggerations are removed, it offers a simplified model with which we may compare some of the things which actually happen when a language is being used. In any case, this is the assumption I shall be working on in this paper.

Verbs and Activities. It can be given a somewhat more linguistic turn. Actions and activities are in our language typically represented by verbs. As a consequence, an answer to the question: "What activities constitute the natural environment of a word?" may sometimes be reformulated as an answer to the question: "What verbs are there to which the word in question has an especially intimate logical rela-

---

[8] For operationalism, cf. e.g., the symposium on "The Present State of Operationalism" in *The Validation of Scientific Theories*, ed. by Philip G. Frank (Boston, 1955).

D

tion ?"[9] Of course, it cannot be assumed that this reformulation is viable in all cases nor assumed that for every word there is but one verb to which it is related logically. For instance, the word which has probably been studied more than any other philosophically interesting word, the word "good," has several different verbs associated with it in this manner. They include the verbs "to evaluate," "to grade," "to praise," "to commend," "to recommend," and "to appreciate."[10] On a given occasion, a statement which contains the word "good" can perhaps be paraphrased in terms of one of these verbs, but no single one of them enables us to reformulate (in context) all the sentences containing the word "good." It is also obvious that if the activities which are expressed by the verbs just listed would cease, the word "good" would lose much of its use and in a sense therefore much of its meaning. There is thus a logical connection between the word "good" and the verbs listed, a connection which is the more interesting the more clearly the paraphrases we can obtain in terms of these verbs bring out the logical conditions of the use of the word "good."

Verbs for Quantifiers. It seems to me that there is an even more interesting instance of this in the philosophy of logic. There are verbs which are not merely logical relatives of the quantifiers "there is," and "for all," but which are veritable next of kin of theirs. These verbs are not to be found among the verbs a philosopher is apt to think in connection with logic, for instance, not among the verbs "to infer," "to follow," "to deduce," "to contradict," and "to refute."[11] In no important case can a quantifier be paraphrased in terms of them, although interesting attempts have been made to connect the most important rules for operating with quantifiers with the notions of inference and deduction.[12]

---

[9] The multiplicity and variety of the different language-games which are involved in the use of language partly explains the Protean character of the grammatical category of verbs. The variety in the logical functions of different verbs is in fact much greater than one would gather from most logical and philosophical discussions of the different grammatical categories.

[10] Cf. R. M. Hare, *The Language of Morals* (Oxford, 1952), and Paul Ziff, *Semantic Analysis* (Ithaca, 1960), last chapter.

[11] Cf. P. F. Strawson, *op. cit.*, pp. 1–4, 15–25.

[12] Notice that one cannot teach the meanings of quantifiers as a radically new idea by listing e.g., semantic truth conditions. The learner must know the metalanguage in which these truth-conditions are formulated. These formulations will themselves turn on the use of the quantifiers of the metalanguage. Hence the most that one can accomplish in this way is to teach the meaning of quantifiers in one language in terms of the quantifiers of another language. From our point of view, to convey the meaning of quantifiers to someone as a radically new idea is to teach him to play the language-games that go together with quantifiers, and to teach him the relation of the different quantifying expressions to these games.

There are much better candidates for the role, namely, such verbs as "to search," "to look for," "to seek," and "to find." In more than one natural language, existence is in fact expressed by speaking of what "can be found" (cf. e.g., the Swedish phrase "det finns" which literally taken means just this). E. Gilson writes that according to Averroës, "the Arabic word meaning 'to exist' came from a root originally meaning 'found', because it seems to have been a common notion that, for any given thing, to exist meant approximately 'to be found there'."[13] In the everyday parlance of mathematicians, existence is typically expressed in this way. It is also obvious enough that instead of "there are black swans" we can in many contexts say "one can find black swans," and, instead of "all swans are white," one can sometimes say "no swans can be found which are not white." One "language-game" in which quantifiers can naturally occur is what I shall call the language-game of seeking and finding; and it seems to me that this is by far the most important kind of language-game in which they can occur. In this respect, the case of quantifiers is different from that of the word "good" which can occur in the context of many different types of activity none of which seems much more interesting logically than the others.

Caveats. There are of course, circumstances in which quantified sentences cannot naturally be rewritten in terms of seeking and finding. "There are mountains on the Moon" is more naturally paraphrased as "One can see mountains on the Moon" than as "One can find mountains on the Moon." In this case, coming to know the existence of the objects in question is a matter of direct observation and therefore ill-suited to the verbs "to seek" or "to search" which normally suggest that some amount of effort and of shifting one's point of view is needed. It is important to realize, however, that ascertaining the existence of individual objects by direct observation is a very special case of coming to know the existence of individuals. What is apt to mislead one is that in the most typical cases a search terminates in a situation in which one is confronted by a directly observable object. However, this does not make it true to say that the existence of the object in question was discovered by direct observation, for that would entirely overlook what seems to be the most important element in the situation, viz. the activities of seeking or

---

[13] Etienne Gilson, *The Christian Philosophy of St. Thomas Aquinas* (London, 1957), p. 39.

52 STUDIES IN LOGICAL THEORY

trying to find.[14] Saying that we always come to know the existence of
individual objects by sensible perception is like saying that one comes
to London from New York by bus when what one means is that one
flies over and then takes a bus to London from the airport.

It can also be pointed out that when the situations are described
more closely in which we allegedly become aware of the existence of
certain objects merely by witnessing them, we very often find ourselves
using words that are closely similar logically to words for searching
and seeking. In order to see an object which is at hand, it does not
always suffice to open one's eyes; we very often have to scan our visual
field even though we do not have to move ourselves from place to
place bodily. Words like "scan" are obviously related to words for
seeking and searching. (Scanning as *visual* searching.)[15]

There is also an opposite type of case in which a paraphrase of a
quantified sentence in terms of searching and finding does not sit
quite happily. It may be illustrated by the sentence "there are transuranium elements" which it would be a little awkward to paraphrase
as "one can find transuranic elements." What misfires here is the
fact that to speak simply of seeking and finding often suggests that no
highly technical methods are required to get at the entities in question.
It is more natural to say e.g., that one can produce transuranium elements. It is of some interest to note that paraphrases in terms of seeking and finding become perceptibly less awkward if the methods used
are specified, thus eliminating the source of awkwardness. It is
perfectly natural to say, for instance, that transuranium elements were
found by such-and-such methods.

In general, the words "to seek" and "to find" apply most aptly to
the middle range of cases in which an effort has to be made to become
aware of the existence (or non-existence) in question but in which no
greatly sophisticated procedures are needed. We may of course
imagine circumstances in which this middle range of cases becomes
increasingly less important. Then verbs other than "to seek" and "to

[14] For the conceptual situation, the crucial question is perhaps not whether one's
mind is a "ghost in a machine" which can only receive messages from the external
world through the receptive mechanisms of the "machine," but whether the mind
can actually move the machine around so as to have a choice of what it can or
cannot perceive. The possibility of active operations on one's environment at will
seems to be deeply imbedded in our conceptual structure, although in some
curious way it gets eliminated in our conscious experience. On this point, cf.
Eino Kaila, "Die konzeptuellen und perzeptuellen Komponenten der Alltagserfah-
rung," *Acta Philosophica Fennica*, vol. 13 (1962), especially pp. 71–73.
[15] I find that Kurt Baier makes use of this very word in his discussion of the
concept of existence. See "Existence," *Proceedings of the Aristotelian Society*,
vol. 61 (1960–1961), pp. 19–40, especially p. 24.

find" might become more important for the meaning of the quantifying expressions of the language in question.

These qualifications nevertheless do not seriously reflect on the importance of the two verbs for appreciating the logic of quantifying expressions. It may be that quantifiers are sometimes better served by the verb "to produce" than by "to find," but many of the relevant logical features of these two verbs are closely similar. Nor do our qualifications sever the discussion from what we find in ordinary discourse. In natural language existence and universality are often expressed by speaking of the outcomes of different courses of action. A case in point is the German idiom "es gibt" whose origin is betrayed by such sentences as "Wenn du hingehst, so gibt es Unglück" (meaning literally: "if you go there, 'it gives' misfortune"—an example listed in Hermann Paul's *Wörterbuch*). In the informal jargon of mathematicians, universality is often expressed by such phrases as "no matter which number you take . . ." The exceptional cases in which "to seek" and "to find" do not give us very natural paraphrases of the quantifiers may even be considered, for our limited purposes, as special cases of seeking and finding in an extended sense. Direct observation is a "trivial case" of finding, and the discovery of an object by a complicated technical procedure may perhaps be considered as the issue of a search conducted by very special means. In this extended sense, it may thus be said that all our knowledge of the existence of external objects is obtained by means of the activities of seeking and finding.

Quantifiers Not Operationalistically Interpretable. In a sense, the meaning of quantifiers is thus their role ("use") in the language-games of seeking and finding, with all the qualifications which I have indicated. On this view, a statement containing quantifiers is comparable with a prediction concerning the outcome of certain processes of searching. These processes are the processes of seeking which we would have to carry out in order to verify the sentence in question. Of course, nothing is said of how these procedures should be conducted. One is also abstracting from all the contingent limitations of our actual capacity of search. Thus the processes of seeking and finding are not "operations" of the kind an operationalistic theory of meaning envisages. One can almost say that, on the contrary, the notions of existence and universality receive their importance from the fact that all the individuals that are known to exist cannot be produced by "operations" whose course is determined in advance. In so far as there is an effective method of verifying or falsifying existential sentences, there is little point in using these sentences. If there were such a method, existential sentences could be replaced by sentences which speak of the particular instances of the claimed existence which are *per hypothesis* obtainable.

How deeply this uncertainty about the outcome of seeking and finding really cuts is indicated by the undecidability of quantification theory. What this undecidability means may be roughly explained by saying that one cannot always predict how far one would have to go in an attempted model set construction in order to bring out the possible inconsistency which may lurk in the set which we are trying to imbed in a model set. In another paper I shall argue that there is a certain analogy between the processes of model set construction and the activities of seeking and finding which one has to perform in verifying or falsifying sentences.[16] In view of this analogy, we may perhaps say that the processes of seeking and finding are as unpredictable as model set constructions.

Furthermore, there usually are many alternative ways of trying to construct a model set for a given set of sentences. Correspondingly, there usually are many alternative ways of trying to verify a sentence by looking for suitable individuals. It is impossible to give general rules as to which alternative will yield a model set, if such there be. Likewise, there does not seem to be much hope of telling which one of many alternative ways of looking for individuals, which would verify a given sentence, is the likeliest one to produce results. In some sense, the activities of seeking and finding therefore present irreducible alternatives. All this shows how far a cry the activities of seeking and looking for are from the operations which an operationalist is willing to countenance.

Language-Games as Games Proper. One way of explaining my theory of what it means to understand quantifiers is to say that according to it one can understand quantifiers if one knows how to play certain kinds of *games*. Whatever there is to be said of the use of the Wittgen-

---

[16] For the concept of a model set, see e.g., Jaakko Hintikka, "A Program and a Set of Concepts for Philosophical Logic," *The Monist*, vol. 51 (1967), pp. 69–92 and "Form and Content in Quantification Theory," *Acta Philosophica Fennica*, vol. 8 (1955), pp. 5–55. Model sets may be thought of as partial descriptions of possible states of affairs; they are consistent, and any consistent set of first-order sentences can be imbedded in at least one of them. A suitable complete proof procedure for first-order logic can be thought of as a method of trying to construct such a description for $\sim F$. If this attempt comes to a dead end, we have proved F. To decide whether F is provable, we thus have to know how far an attempted counter-example construction has to proceed in order to bring out whatever inconsistency there may lurk in $\sim F$. Because a decision procedure is impossible, we know that this cannot be recursively predicted. This unpredictability of model set constructions illustrates vividly the tremendous difference between them and the predictable operations of the operationalists.

steinian term "language-game" in general, here the word "game" at any rate sits especially happily. This happiness is not only due to whatever informal similarities there are between games proper and those activities which Gilbert Ryle has called "the game of exploring the world."[17] It is primarily due to the fact that in the case of quantifiers, the relevant "language-games" can also be formulated as games in the precise game-theoretical sense of the word.

In these games, one's opponent can be thought of in different ways: he may be simply nature, but he may also be some recalcitrant *malin genie* making the most of his chances of frustrating us. The game is most easily explained in the case of sentences in the prenex normal form (initial string of quantifiers followed by a "matrix" which does not contain any quantifiers). Since all quantificational sentences (classically interpreted) can be converted into this form, the explanation of the "game" that goes together with such a sentence will be in effect rather general.

My end in the game is to make a substitution-instance of the matrix true. My opponent's ("nature's") aim is to make the outcome of the game to be a false substitution-instance of the matrix. Each existential quantifier marks my move: I choose (produce, find) an individual whose name is to be substituted for the corresponding bound variable.[18] Each universal quantifier marks a move by my opponent: he is free to produce an individual whose name is to be substituted for the variables bound to the universal quantifier. The order of the moves corresponds to the order of the quantifiers.

It is readily seen that quite a few things which are ordinarily expressed by speaking of quantified sentences can be expressed by speaking of the correlated games. For instance, for a sentence to be true it is necessary and sufficient that I have (as a matter of fact) a winning strategy in the correlated game, in the sense of game theory.[19]

On the other hand, it is quite clear that the games which this interpretation associates with quantificational sentences are to all intents and purposes tantamount to the games ("language-games") of looking for and finding. The imaginary opponent merely serves to highlight our own attempts to make sure that certain kinds of counter-examples

---

[17] Gilbert Ryle, "Sensations" in *Contemporary British Philosophy*, Third Series, ed. by H. D. Lewis (London, 1956), p. 442.

[18] Notice that this individual need not have a name prior to a move of this kind.

[19] See R. Duncan Luce and Howard Raiffa, *Games and Decisions* (New York, 1957) or Anatol Rapoport, *Two-Person Game Theory: The Essential Ideas* (Ann Arbor, 1966).

cannot be found (that the opponent "cannot defeat us"). Hence our interpretation does in a sense bring out all there is to be brought out in the logic of quantification.

The naturalness of the game-theoretic point of view is illustrated by the fact that this interpretation is sometimes resorted to spontaneously by writers who are explaining the meaning of quantifiers in non-systematic contexts. Developed more systematically, it has been employed by Leon Henkin, not only to explain the meaning of the usual kind of quantification, but to extend it further in one direction.[20]

Notice that the question as to what the individual moves are to be *called* is left open by the game-theoretic interpretation which I have sketched. The applicability of whatever term we want to use will depend on the details of the situation. In one of them, seeking and finding may be the most apt words; in another, producing might be a better one. In this respect, the game-theoretic interpretation is neutral with respect to the choice between these different descriptive expressions. It also brings out the fact that this choice is largely immaterial for my purposes, for clearly the games in question have the same character (same structure) no matter what the procedures are *called* that lead me to choose one individual rather than another. Hence many of the language-games which I have called games of seeking and finding might be as well (and better) called something else. All this is closely related to what I said earlier of the applicability of the various words of the natural language to the language-games in question.

The games just described are in many ways closely related to the systematic theory of quantification, and might even open possibilities of generalizing it. Some possibilities and some results that have already been reached in this direction are indicated in the appendix. Here I shall only explain how the game-theoretic interpretation can be extended to sentences which are not in the prenex form. Again the game proceeds from the whole sentence to substitution-instances of its subsentences. My aim is to end up with a true atomic sentence. The rules for quantifiers remain the same. Disjunction now marks my move: I have to choose a disjunct with reference to which the game is continued. Conjunction marks a move by my opponent: he chooses

[20] See Leon Henkin, "Some Remarks on Infinitely Long Formulas" in *Infinitistic Methods*. Proceedings of a Symposium on Foundations of Mathematics (Warsaw, 1961), pp. 176–183. For a further development of Henkin's observations, see J. H. Keisler, "Finite Approximations of Infinitely Long Formulas" in *The Theory of Models, Proceedings of the 1963 International Symposium at Berkeley*, ed. by J. W. Addison, Leon Henkin and Alfred Tarski (Amsterdam, 1965), pp. 158–169 especially pp. 160–161.

a conjunct with reference to which the game is continued. Negation $\sim F$ has the effect of changing the roles of the players, after which the game continues by reference to F. This serves to define the game correlated with any quantificational sentence, assuming that a domain of individuals is given with the appropriate predicates defined on this domain.

The games which are thus correlated with quantificational sentences are closely connected with the activities by means of which one can try to verify these sentences. As far as my own moves are concerned, precisely the same things are involved in the verification of quantificational sentences and in the games we have correlated with them. In the case of my opponent's moves, I have to make sure that I cannot be defeated by any of his strategies. This can be thought of as involving a temporary switch of roles: I have to play the role of the devil's (or the nature's) advocate—that is, the role of my opponent—for a while in order to see what possibilities he has of defeating me. This is neatly reflected by the possibility of replacing the universal quantifier $(\forall x)$ by $\sim(\exists x)\sim$, which eliminates my opponent's move but involves a temporary exchange of roles.

With this proviso, the games I have described are in effect the activities by means of which one can try to verify quantificational sentences. By describing these games in some detail one can thus see what the activities are of whose outcomes we are making, as it were, a prediction when we assert a quantificational sentence. All this illustrated the close logical connection which (I am arguing) there is between quantifiers and the "games" of looking for and finding.

Presuppositions of the Language-Games of Seeking and Finding. The justification for this connection must lie to a considerable extent in the light which this connection throws on the logical behavior of the quantifying expressions of ordinary language and of formal logic. Does it throw any such light?

If quantifiers go together with the verbs "to seek," "to look for," and "to find," the conditions for the significant (or, as some students of language would like us to say, non-deviant) use of quantifiers must be approximately the same as the conditions for the use of these verbs. Now what is required for the notions of seeking and looking for to make sense? Two main requirements obviously have to be met. First, the field of search must somehow be defined, however partially. Second, there must be ways of ascertaining when one has found the individual or the kind of individual one has been looking for. These are obviously also requirements that have to be satisfied in order for the games properly described above to be playable.

I shall call these requirements the first and the second requirement. Both of them are relevant to the logical behavior of quantifying expressions in ordinary language and in the formal systems of logic. We shall examine them in the order in which they were mentioned.

The first requirement helps us to understand, *inter alia*, why unqualified statements of existence are apt to strike one as odd (deviant). We are likely to find any number of perfectly natural utterances of the form "there are chairs upstairs," or "there is an infinity of prime numbers," but it is doubtful whether we can find many non-deviant utterances of the form "there are numbers" or "there are chairs" outside the philosophers' discussions.

It is now easy to see what is wrong with these unqualified statements. Part of the function of the missing qualification is to indicate what this field of search is: hence the meaning of these statements is incomplete, and can only be gathered from the context at best.

It is interesting to note that a very small change alters the situation radically. The statement "there are black swans" is perfectly in order, as might indeed be expected from our point of view. In this statement the class of swans constitutes the relevant field of search, or part of it, which is taken to be given clearly enough for the operations of seeking and finding to make sense. Attention is concentrated, so to speak, on the additional question whether within this well-defined universe of discourse one can find swans of a particular color.

There is an interesting asymmetry here between positive and negative statements. Although sentences like "there are swans" are very often awkward to utter, similar negative statements like "there are no dodos" are perfectly in order. Again an explanation is forthcoming. In an unqualified negative statement the field of search does not matter (if it does, the statement is dangerously vague), and hence the need for specifying it is much smaller than is the corresponding positive statement. These, in turn, can lose their awkwardness when contrasted to a real or imagined effort to deny the existence of the individuals in question. As Peter Geach has urged on me,[21] there is nothing wrong with a sentence like "there *are* swans, and they really are ugly in their first year, just as Hans Andersen says."

The same point emerges also from the observation of other quantifying expressions of ordinary language. Such words as "some," "any," and "all" are, in Austin's phrase, substantive-hungry. No matter whether the statement "there are swans" makes sense or not, it cannot be paraphrased in terms of "some" without bringing in new

---

[21] Private communication.

words which serve to indicate the relevant field of search, for instance, "Some extant birds are swans." The words "some" and "any" occur in such constructions as "some X" or "some X's" and "any X," where X is a general noun. Part of the function of this general noun, and a reason why it is needed, is to indicate the field of search which is being presupposed. Where such a field of search or part of it is available, these words can be used. Thus "There are black swans," becomes "Some swans are black." A statement like "All ravens are black" is therefore not quite accurately translated into the language of formal logic by "$(\forall x)(x$ is a raven $\supset x$ is black)," for in this translation some definitely given large universe of discourse is being presupposed while in the original the extent of the underlying field of search was left largely unspecified, the only relevant assumption being that it must include all ravens.[22]

Often the exact boundaries of the field of search are not clearly defined; there is a similar vagueness in the meaning of the corresponding quantified sentences. Austin once posed the question (it was one of the problems which have been published in *Analysis*) whether the statement "All swans are white" refers to whatever swans there may be on the canals of Mars.[23] As emerged from the answers, there is a complication here in that the inductive evidence on which we may think of the statement to be based may tacitly restrict its scope to terrestial swans. Apart from this complication, however, the statement serves to illustrate the vagueness I have in mind.

Formal logicians usually assume that all the different fields of search can be happily pooled together into one big "universe of discourse." There may be reasons for this complacency, but the situation would merit a closer look. The difficulty of pooling different fields of search together does not lie primarily in the dissimilarity of the entities which thus have to be treated as equal. A more important problem is due to the fact that there may be interdependencies between individuals in the different fields of search. One may look for rivers of different kinds, and one may look for waters of different kinds. However, there cannot exist rivers without there also existing waters.[24]

---

[22] For a detailed discussion of a number of problems in this area (from a somewhat different point of view), see Ernest W. Adams, "Probability and the Logic of Conditionals" in *Aspects of Inductive Logic*, ed. by Jaakko Hintikka and Patrick Suppes (Amsterdam, 1966), pp. 265–316.

[23] See J. L. Austin, "Report on Analysis 'Problem' No. 12," *Analysis*, vol. 18 (1957–1958), pp. 97–101 (with two "solutions" to the problem).

[24] Cf. Peter Geach, *Reference and Generality* (Ithaca, 1962), and W.V.O. Quine, "Unification of Universes in Set Theory," *The Journal of Symbolic Logic*, vol. 21 (1956), pp. 267–279.

In the applications of logic the frequent indeterminacy of the pertinent field of search is shown especially clearly by the odd results of the process of contraposition. It seems rather odd to paraphrase "every man is selfish" by "no unselfish thing is a man." These two sentences will be logically equivalent as soon as the relevant field of search has been fixed. But the sentences themselves do not specify this field, and they presuppose different things concerning it. "Every man is selfish" presupposes that the class of all men is part of the field of search. "No unselfish thing is a man" presupposes that the totality of unselfish things has been defined clearly enough to be amenable to our activities of seeking and finding. Hence these two sentences do not have the same logical powers in ordinary discourse.

These odd results of contraposition cannot be explained away in the way in which some philosophers have sought to explain away some of the paradoxes of confirmation, that is to say, by reference to the relative sizes of the classes involved. In the case at hand such an attempt would presumably consist of pointing out that there are many more things (and things of many different sorts) which cannot be said to be selfish than there are human beings, and of arguing that this makes it more natural to use the former class as an antecedent of a general implication than the latter. However, this maneuver does not help at all. "No indivisible entity is a material body" is markedly more deviant than "every material body is divisible," all the more so in the mouth of a materialist.

In the same way, the statements "some swans are black" and "some black objects are swans" are not equivalent in ordinary discourse. The former presupposes that the relevant field of search includes all swans, the latter that it includes all black objects.

In relation to the requirement that the field of search is to be delineated, the verb "to produce" behaves somewhat differently from the verb "to look for." The methods of producing an object of a certain kind both with respect to their scope and with respect to the nature of the procedures involved are restricted somewhat less narrowly than the methods of finding one. In this sense, the "field of search" connected with production is wider and more flexible than those connected with searching and finding. This may be part of the reason why it is more natural to say, for instance, "we can produce transuranium elements" or "we can produce neutrinos" than to say, "we can find transuranium elements" or, "we can find neutrinos." Sometimes this difference is connected with doubts about whether the objects produced exist objectively apart from our methods of production. However, even where this is not at issue, the difference between the verbs "to produce" and "to find" is marked enough, as it seems to be in the examples I just gave. All this tends to make the verb "to produce" somewhat more amenable to the purposes of a formal logician, who needs a large, all-comprehensive field of search for his "universe of discourse," than the verb "to find."

End-Points of Search. The second requirement is likewise of considerable interest. In order for the notions of seeking and finding to make sense, and hence for the quantifiers to make sense, we must have some idea of the circumstances in which we can stop and claim to have found what we have been looking for. In brief, the conditions of having found the thing we are looking for must be determined. These may often be defined with reference to the results of further search; i.e., quantifiers may occur within the scope of other quantifiers; but ultimately our conditions will normally specify absolute stopping-points for our search. Of course, the conditions of "really having found" something are not always without a certain vagueness. The paradigmatic case is that of being able to point to a physical object or to a man and to say: "There is one!" But how the other cases shade into this one is not always very clear. However, this vagueness does not sever the logic of seeking and finding from that of existence. The difficulties which there often are in deciding whether entities which we cannot immediately confront (such as a neutrino, a field, or a gene) "really exist" or not are largely difficulties in deciding what is to count as finding or producing one of these entities.[25] As Stephen Toulmin puts it, certain things are generally taken to be sufficient for the purpose of showing the "real existence" of physical entities, "for instance, cloud-chamber pictures of α-rays, electron microscope photographs, or, as a second best, audible clicks from a Geiger counter."[26] The reason why these count as demonstrations of actual existence is that they are, again in Toulmin's words, "sufficiently like being shown a living dodo on the lawn" or, in my terms, sufficiently like the paradigmatic cases of finding an object by directly confronting it. Thus for a working physicist "the question, 'Do neutrinos exist?' acts as an invitation to 'produce a neutrino,' preferably by making it visible"—or, as we may equally well say, to find a neutrino for us to witness.

The second requirement also seems to me to be relevant to the evaluation of a famous "argument" of G. E. Moore. Norman Malcolm

[25] According to some reports, Ernst Mach's standard reply to those who claimed that atoms exist was "Have you seen one?" (I derive this item of information from Stephen Brush, "Mach and Atomism," *Synthese*, vol. 18 (1968).)

[26] Stephen Toulmin, *Philosophy of Science* (London, 1953), pp. 135–137.

has suggested that what looks like arguments in Moore should often be construed as reminders that certain concepts have a logically correct use in our language.[27] On this view, Moore did not have to produce *true* or *paradigmatic* examples of the use of these concepts in order to accomplish his end, although he certainly did try to do so himself. What happens now to this view if it is applied to Moore's famous "proof of the external world"?[28] The crucial concept here is that of existence. What do we have to be reminded of in order to bring it home to us that we can use it impeccably as applied to what Moore calls "external objects" or "objects which are to be met with in space"? It follows from what I have said that there are two main things one has to ascertain in order to make sure that a concept of existence applies to objects of a certain sort; they are incorporated in my first and second requirement. The first is not crucial here, partly because we are dealing with the question whether there are any "external objects" at all. This being so, we are in effect facing a potential denial of the existence of any "external objects" at all, which makes the precise specification of the field of search less crucial in the same way it did in our dodo example earlier.

Hence the main burden falls on the requirement that we must have criteria of having found whatever we are looking for. This requirement in effect says that it must make sense to say, "Now I have found an X" in order for the concept of existence to be applicable to X's. How could one hope to bring home to an audience that we do in fact have such criteria for deciding when we have found "an external object" or have met "an object to be met with in space"? Clearly by staging as paradigmatic an instance of a confrontation with an "external object" as one could imagine. One displays an "external object" and says, "Here is one"; one displays another and says, "Here is another." And this is precisely what Moore does in his "proof of the external world": he waves a hand and says, "Here is a hand."

What Moore does thus receives a perfectly reasonable and indeed predictable sense when seen in the light in which Malcolm wants to view Moore's philosophical activity in general. By enacting his little scene, Moore reminds us that we know perfectly well what it means to be confronted with an "external object" so as to be able to say, "Here

[27] Norman Malcolm, "George Edward Moore" in his *Knowledge and Certainty: Essays and Lectures* (Englewood Cliffs, 1963), pp. 163–183.
[28] G. E. Moore, "Proof of an External World," *Proceedings of the British Academy*, vol. 25 (1939); reprinted in G. E. Moore, *Philosophical Papers* (London, 1959), ch. 7.

is one!" and that one of the main presuppositions of our use of the concept of existence is therefore satisfied. In Moore there is, of course, also the implication that in the ensuing sense of existence, it is indeed obvious that there are "external objects." I would agree with Malcolm, however, that for this purpose Moore's skit is both unnecessary and perhaps even insufficient. It matters little whether on the actual occasion before the British Academy Moore actually succeeded in pointing to his hand or to any other external object.[29] What matters is only the fact that we can in principle do this and that we also often succeed in doing so. Moore is not as much proving the existence of the external world as pointing out that we have in fact an impeccable concept of existence as applied to hands, chairs, houses and other commonplace "external objects."

I am not quite sure whether our concept of existence as applied to commonplace external objects is quite as unproblematic as Moore's argument presupposes (on the construction I have put on it). However, even if it is not, there is a point Moore's argument makes: In so far as we do have a satisfactory idea of what it means for external objects to exist, it must make sense to speak of finding them and confronting them. If we want to criticize the former idea, we have to examine the latter idea more closely.

It may be argued that the interest of Moore's "proof" is difficult to bring out in other ways. For instance, it does not help to ask what Moore was doing when he said, "Here is one hand, and here is another." He certainly was not informing his audience of something they did not know before. Nor is there any other natural purpose in view which his statement could serve. The whole question of the *use* of his statement seems oddly out of place.

Moore's argument cannot be construed as a formal inference, either. We may admit that hands are external objects, but this does not carry us very far. The crucial statement "this is a hand" or "here is a hand" should presumably be taken as a subject-predicate of the form $P(a)$. I have pointed out elsewhere that from this we can only infer $(\exists x)P(x)$ (i.e., "hands exist") if we have an additional premiss of the form $(\exists x)(x=a)$ which ensures that the object referred to by the term a ("this object") exists.[30] However, this is just what we cannot assume here. To assume that the hand Moore is waving really exists

[29] If you have inverting goggles on (of the kind now used in some psychological experiments), then it may actually be difficult for you to point to your hand. Does this make it more difficult for you to "prove the existence of an external world" in Moore's sense?

[30] See Jaakko Hintikka, "On the Logic of Existence and Necessity," *The Monist*, vol. 50 (1966), pp. 55–76.

is to beg the very question he is asking. Hence his argument does not have any validity as a formal proof. We can draw existential conclusions without explicit or hidden existential premises as little as we can derive as "ought" from an "is." Whatever persuasiveness Moore's famous "proof" has derives from its being the kind of paradigmatic confrontation with an external object which we must have in order for the notion of existence to be applicable.

Marking the Different Moves. In order to bring out more fully the connection between quantifying expressions and the activities of seeking and finding and to perceive some of the consequences of this connection it is advisable to consider somewhat more complicated cases. Consider as an example the sentence "Some Englishman has seen all the countries of the world." In order to verify this sentence, we therefore have to fix upon one individual at a time and investigate whether he perhaps satisfies this double requirement. This means that we have to distinguish him, for the time being at least, from the other individuals whom we also have to keep an eye on. If we know his name, we may use it. If not, we may assign some conventional designation to him, like the John Does and Richard Roes of legal parlance. If the context allows, we may also speak simply of *this* man or *that* man. The necessity of distinguishing him from others in some way or another is closely related to our second requirement for the meaningfulness of quantifying expressions. We must have ways of marking the different moves in our game; we must be able to distinguish not only the end-points but also the branching-points of the different possible courses which our interconnected processes of seeking and finding may take. Even if we have already come across an Englishman such as we are looking for, we still have to distinguish him from others while we make sure that he is related to each of the countries of the world in the required way.

This new requirement is closely related to recent disputes concerning the dispensability of free singular terms in favor of mere variables of quantification. (Certain aspects of the controversy cannot be touched here; for instance, the question whether it is possible to teach and to learn a language without free singular terms—a subject of which we all seem to know very little.) The requirement just mentioned is probably part of the truth which there seems to be in the contention of those who think of singular terms as being indispensable. It is e.g., closely related to the point which Mr. P. F. Strawson has expressed by saying "there could not be a form of words having the meaning 'There is something or other which has attribute *A*' unless there were also a form of words having the meaning '*This* thing has attribute A'."[31] We must, in fact, have, it seems, some ways of referring to one particular individual rather than to others for a while at least, in order for the language-games of seeking and finding to be practicable and hence for quantifying expressions to make sense.

This much is certainly true. However, certain other contentions of the defenders of free singular terms do not follow from it. For instance, it does not follow that there is something in the actual body of our knowledge which we cannot express in terms of quantifiers and bound variables although we can express it by means of free singular terms.

It does not follow, either, that there must be a category of proper names, demonstratives, or other free singular terms in one's language. We must require that there are ways of marking the end-points and other crucial junctures of our interlocking processes of search, processes which are (*inter alia*) required for the verification of sentences with more than one layer of quantifiers. Consider the simplest case as an example. This is what was called the second requirement. It says that the end-points of search must be somehow recognizable. This recognition must of course be marked in the language-game in question. It may be the case that we can simply say: "*This* is the kind of object we have been looking for" (say one with the attribute A). It does not follow, however, that we must be able to mark the end-points by *saying* of the particular object we have reached that it has the attribute A. Instead of saying anything about this particular individual we might say in general terms "Now we know that there is an object with the attribute A." Of course, in order for such utterances to serve to mark the end-points of search we must have some nonverbal means of making it known that we assert the existence of at least one individual of the appropriate kind on the basis of witnessing that particular individual we actually witnessed. From the necessity of employing such nonverbal devices of communication it does not follow, however, that there must be an expression in the language which can serve this purpose. Turning Strawson's formulation around, we might say that there need not be any *form of words* having the meaning "This thing has attribute A" in a language although the language in question contains a form of words having the meaning "there is something with the attribute A."

[31] Cf. W. V. O. Quine, *Methods of Logic* (New York, 1950), pp. 220–224; W. V. O. Quine, *From a Logical Point of View* (Cambridge, Mass., 1953), pp. 7–8, 13, 146 and 166–167; W. V. O. Quine, *Word and Object* (Cambridge, Mass., 1960), pp. 179–186; P. F. Strawson, "Singular Terms and Predication," *The Journal of Philosophy*, vol. 58 (1961), pp. 393–412; P. F. Strawson, *Individuals* (London, 1959), pp. 199–203; P. F. Strawson, "Singular Terms, Ontology, and Identity," *Mind*, vol. 65 (1956), pp. 433–454.

E

However, there must be some alternative way of indicating the same thing, that is to say, of bringing out what the former expresses over and above the latter. There must be nonverbal means to call one's attention to particular individuals even though there need not be verbal means for doing so.[32]

General Morals. There is also a general moral or two to be drawn from our observations. If there really obtains the close relationship between quantifiers and the activities of searching and trying to find, we have a stronger reason than ever to be suspicious of the Carnapian methods which have been criticized in some of my earlier papers.[33] The use of these methods sometimes presupposes, it was argued, that all the individuals in the universe of discourse are known. In any case, not very much attention is paid in these methods to the discovery and introduction of new individuals. If the use of quantifiers is essentially connected with the activities of seeking and finding new individuals, we cannot hope that any methods which make no provision for such activities will throw much light on the logic of quantification. It seems to me significant that some of the main theoretical difficulties to which the application of Carnapian methods lead arise in connection with quantified sentences.

To conclude with another general point: We can perhaps now see one partial reason for the interest of the formal logic of quantification. If it is true that the processes of seeking and finding are the most important processes by means of which we become aware of the existence of individuals, and if it is also true that the language-games of seeking and finding are the natural context of quantifiers, then the study of the logical behavior of quantifiers is largely a study of the structure of some of the most important processes by means of which we obtain our knowledge. It is perhaps worth noting that the formal logic of quantification can have this interest independently of how closely it reproduces the ways in which we in the natural language refer to the activities of seeking and finding. As a brief *dictum* we might perhaps say this: Quantification theory is a regimented way of speaking of the activities of seeking and finding. It is not a regimentation of the ways in which we speak of these activities in *ordinary language*. If quantification theory helps us to carry out the processes of seeking and finding or at the very least helps us to clear up our

---

[32] It may also be the case that it is in many cases *practically* impossible to get along with nonverbal means only. I do not see, however, any general logical argument for not being able to do so in some cases.

[33] Jaakko Hintikka, "Are Logical Truths Tautologies?" in *Deskription, Analytizität und Existenz*, ed. by P. Weingartner (Munich and Salzburg, 1966), pp. 215–233. (See especially pp. 221–223).

ideas concerning them, it has an interesting application even if it should turn out not to apply very well to a direct study and regimentation of ordinary language. In a sequel to this paper I shall try to bring out at least one way in which the formal logic of quantification helps us with our language-games of seeking and finding. The "thought" we carry out in formal logic will turn out to be relevant to the non-linguistic "action" in a clear-cut fashion.

APPENDIX:

LANGUAGE-GAMES AND SYSTEMATIC LOGICAL THEORY

Although the game-theoretic point of view on first-order logic which was sketched in the body of this paper apparently has never been discussed in its full generality before, it is obviously closely related to a number of issues and approaches in systematic logical theory. Here only a few relatively informal remarks will be made to illustrate the naturalness and importance of the connection between the logic of quantification and the games of searching and looking for.

The game-theoretic approach is closely related to the idea of eliminating quantifiers in favor of functions and functionals, and to the basic idea of the so-called "no counter-example interpretation."[34] For instance, there is obviously a very close connection between the truth of a statement of the form

(I) $(\exists x)\ (\forall y)(\exists z)\ F(x,y,z)$

where the variables are assumed to range over natural numbers, and the statement

(II) $(\exists x)(\exists f)(\forall y)F(x,y,f(x))$

with a function variable f. This function and a number x are precisely what determines "my" strategy in the game correlated with (I). Hence the force of (II) is in effect to say that there is a winning strategy in the game correlated with (I). If a suitable x and f can in fact be given, the existential quantifiers in (II) can be dropped, leaving us with a quantifier-free statement.[35]

I shall not discuss how simple observations of this sort are utilized

<hr />

[34] See William Tait, "The Substitution Method," *The Journal of Symbolic Logic*, vol. 30 (1965), pp. 175–192.
[35] For a brief survey of a number of developments in this direction, see Andrzej Mostowski, "Thirty Years of Foundational Studies," *Acta Philosophica Fennica*, vol. 17 (1966), lecture IV.

in the "no counter-example interpretation" or in other developments in logical theory. I have merely tried to illustrate the main idea, which seems clear enough: We take a sentence or formula (e.g., a number-theoretic one), correlate with it a game along the lines indicated, and then express by an explicit statement the fact that there is a winning strategy in this game. This new statement will then serve as an interpretation of the original sentence or formula.

This general technique admits of many variations. One may try to consider, not the game correlated with a statement, but rather the game correlated with its negation. If games of infinite length are used, we may require that they have to be won in a finite number of moves, and so on. Perhaps the most important variation is the possibility of choosing the strategy set in different ways.

If f is allowed to range over *arbitrary* (number-theoretical) functions in our example, (II) is true if and only if (I) is true in the classical arithmetic. It lies very close at hand, however, to suggest that the class of pure strategies we "really" have available is narrower than that. This means restricting the range of the function quantifier in (II). For instance, it might appear natural to let f range over recursive functions only. (How could anyone actually use a strategy given by a non-recursive function?) This will correspond to some nonclassical sense of truth and falsity for (I).[36] In this way, we can perhaps see with some clarity what it could mean actually to employ a nonclassical logic in one's "games of exploring the world": it could mean to use a restricted pure strategy set in the game correlated with (I). Alternatively, or in addition to this, the use of a nonclassical conception of logic could also mean defining the moves of the game which are con nected with the different connectives and quantifiers in a way different from the characterizations of these moves given earlier.

It seems to me that a number of approaches and arguments in the foundational studies might become more accessible to a philosophical scrutiny when looked upon from this game-theoretic point of view, although their precise connections with the game-theoretical concepts and ideas often remain to be worked out.

The following observation has struck me as being especially suggestive: There is a very close connection between the concept of a truth-value of a sentence and the game-theoretical concept of the value of the correlated game. If I have a winning strategy, the value of the game is the payoff of winning, i.e., the "value" of winning the game. This is also precisely the case in which the sentence is true. Hence the

---

[36] Of course, the interpretation of the sentential connectives is also important here.

payoff of winning as a value of the game can be identified with the truth-value "true" of the sentence, and correspondingly for falsity.

It follows that the fact that classical logic is two-valued is virtually tantamount to the fact that the games correlated with classically interpreted statements like (I) admit of pure optimal strategies. That this should be the case is not quite immediate, for in the case of an infinite domain the games have infinite (pure) strategy sets. The existence of pure optimal strategies nevertheless follows from well-known general results which rely essentially on the fact that we are dealing with games with perfect information.

However, if suitable changes are made in our assumptions, optimal strategies (if any) might turn out to be mixed. The weights of the different pure strategies involved in this mixture could then perhaps serve as models of nonclassical truth-values.

This idea remains to be explored, as far as I know. However, it is obvious that there are extant theories which could be, and perhaps have been, conceived of in a game-theoretic spirit. One example among many is Gödel's suggested extension of the finitistic point of view.[37] Here each arithmetical statement is interpreted in terms of another one which can be taken to be essentially a statement to the effect that a certain game correlated with the first statement has a winning strategy. The pure strategy sets are assumed to be restricted to those than can be defined by means of recursive functions and functionals.

Furthermore, a not insubstantial amount of important systematic work in the model theory of first-order logic either has been or can readily be described in game-theoretic terms. Here I shall give only a few indications of some of the results that have been reached. In the application of game theoretic ideas just outlined, a game is connected with each statement, interpreted so as to speak of a certain piece of world or of a "model." Two such models are said to be elementarily equivalent if and only if they are equivalent with respect to all the different games we have described. Now Ehrenfeucht and Fraïssé have in effect shown how for the purpose of describing elementary equivalence this variety of games can be replaced by a single game of comparing the two models.[38] In this game, a move by my opponent (who

[37] Kurt Gödel, "Über eine bisher noch nicht benutzte Erweiterung des finiten Standpunktes," *Dialectica*, vol. 12 (1958), pp. 76–83.
[38] A. Ehrenfeucht, "An Application of Games to the Completeness Problem for Formalized Theories," *Fundamenta Mathematicae*, vol. 49 (1960–1961), pp. 129–141; R. Fraïssé, "Sur quelques classifications des relations basées sur des isomorphismes restraintes," *Publications Scientifiques de l'Université d'Alger*, Serie A, vol. 2 (1955), pp. 15–60 and pp. 273–295.

has the first move) consists in picking out an individual a from one of the two models, say M (of his own choosing). My next move consists in trying to choose from the other model M' an individual a' whose relations to those members of M' which have been picked out earlier match the relations of a to the corresponding members of M and whose attributes match the attributes of a. If I cannot do this, I lose; if I do not lose after any finite number of moves, I win. Then M and M' are elementarily equivalent if and only if I have a winning strategy in the game so defined.

It turns out that this game, and all the truncated versions one obtains by restricting both players to a finite number of moves, are connected very closely with what I have called distributive normal forms and discussed elsewhere in some detail.[39] For instance, I have a winning strategy in the truncated game with precisely d moves for each player if and only if the same constituent with depth d is true both in M and in M'. Then (and only then) the two models M and M' are also equivalent for the purposes of all games correlated with statements of depth d or less. (Depth is roughly speaking characterized as the number of layers of quantifiers in a sentence.) In certain other respects, too, a consideration of constituents helps us to appreciate the close connection which there obtains between the games of comparing two different models and the games correlated with statements.

These examples perhaps suffice to illustrate my suggestion that the logic of quantification is essentially the logic of certain kinds of games of seeking and finding (or whatever you want to call them).

The most systematic earlier use of game-theoretical ideas in quantification theory is due to Paul Lorenzen and developed further by Wolfgang Stegmüller and K. Lorenz (*inter alia*).[40] Some connections between their approach and the above remarks are obvious. However,

[39] Jaakko Hintikka, "Distributive Normal Forms in First-Order Logic" in *Formal Systems and Recursive Functions*, ed. by J. N. Crossley and M. A. E. Dummett (Amsterdam, 1965), pp. 47–90; Jaakko Hintikka, "Distributive Normal Forms and Deductive Interpolation," *Zeitschrift für mathematische Logik und Grundlagen der Mathematik*, vol. 10 (1964), pp. 185–191. The truncated versions of the comparison-game are also very closely related to the games which were correlated with distributive normal forms in the first place.

[40] See Paul Lorenzen, "Ein dialogisches Konstruktivitätskriterium" in *Infinitistic Methods*, Proceedings of a Symposium on Foundations of Mathematics (Warsaw, 1961); Paul Lorenzen, *Metamathematik* (Mannheim, 1962); K. Lorenz, *Arithmetik und Logik als Spiele* (Doctoral Dissertation, Kiel, 1961); K. Lorenz, "Dialogspiele als semantische Grundlage von Logikkalkülen," *Archiv für mathematische Logik und Grundlagenforschung* (forthcoming); Wolfgang Stegmüller, "Remarks on the Completeness of Logical Systems Relative to the Validity-Concepts of P. Lorenzen and K. Lorenz," *Notre Dame Journal of Formal Logic*, vol. 5 (1964), pp. 81–112.

there is also a difference which from a philosophical point of view is very important. The games I have described are related to the uses of logical symbols in finding out something about the world. They are not "indoor games"; they are "played" in the wide world among whatever objects our statements speak about. An essential part of all these games consists in trying to find individuals which satisfy certain requirements.

In contrast to our games of seeking and finding, the games of Lorenzen and Stegmüller are "dialogical games" which are played so to speak "indoors" by means of verbal "challenges" and "responses." These may be made e.g., by writing down suitable sequences of symbols.

As was already pointed out, there are of course very close connections between the formal games of Lorenzen and Stegmüller and the games which I have described and which have been called language-games. If one is merely interested in suitable technical problems in logic, there may not be much to choose between the two types of games. However, from a philosophical point of view, the difference seems to be absolutely crucial. Only considerations which pertain to "games of exploring the world" can be hoped to throw any light on the role of our logical concepts in the meaningful use of language.[41]

In fact, it seems to me that a sharp distinction has to be made between such "outdoor" games of exploring the world in order to verify or falsify certain (interpreted) statements by producing suitable individuals and such "indoor" games as e.g., proving that certain uninterpreted formulae are logical truths by manipulating sequences of symbols in a suitable way. Unless this distinction is made, the relevance of games of the latter type cannot be satisfactorily described. In another paper, I shall try to show in what way the formal language-game of proving or disproving quantificational formulae can help us in the "field games" of trying to verify or falsify quantificational statements.

If there is anything to be learned from the possibility of applying game-theoretic concepts to the systematic theory of first-order logic, it is that the study of the *use* of a language (or a part of a language) can be as purely logical and philosophical an enterprise as the study of logical syntax or the study of the referential relations between language and the world. It seems to me that the familiar Carnapian trichotomy syntax-semantics-pragmatics is often misunderstood to imply that all the study of language in use (as distinguished from its

---

[41] Cf. also Georg Kreisel's comments in his forthcoming review of Lorenzen, "Ein dialogisches Konstruktivitätskriterium."

formal aspects and from its referential relations to the world) belongs to the psychology and sociology of language or to some such non-philosophical and nonlogical discipline.[42] Without wanting to detract from the interest and importance of these studies, it ought to be clear that the use of language can be studied in abstraction from the psychological and sociological conditions of the people using it quite as well as syntax can be studied in abstraction from the psychological make-up and social context of the people who write or utter the sentences whose syntax we are studying. (Of course, this is not to say that important factual connections might be found in both cases.) The study of the games correlated with quantificational sentences perhaps serves to illustrate the possibility and interest of such purely logical pragmatics.

University of Helsinki
AND *Stanford University*

[42] Clear examples of this line of thought are found in Colin Cherry, *On Human Communication* (second edition Cambridge, Mass., 1966), p. 223; and in A. Pap, *Semantics, and Necessary Truth* (New Haven, 1958), p. 434. See also Charles Morris, "Pragmatism and Logical Empiricism" in *The Philosophy of Rudolf Carnap*, ed. by P. A. Schilpp (La Salle, 1963), pp. 87–98, especially pp. 88–89. Carnap's reply in the same volume (p. 861) shows that the confusion I am criticizing cannot be attributed to his present position, whatever effects his earlier statements on the subject may have had.

III

Types, Categories, and Nonsense

JAMES W. CORNMAN*

> All [category] propositions are philosophers' proposi-
> tions (not necessarily, of course, of professional or
> paid philosophers), and the converse is also, I think,
> true. (G. Ryle in "Categories.")

IN the above quotation Gilbert Ryle expresses the extreme position
that the only propositions which are peculiarly philosophical are
category propositions, i.e., propositions which assert "something
about the logical type of a factor or set of factors."[1] A less extreme
view, also expressed by Ryle, is that many philosophical doctrines
involve what he calls category mistakes, i.e., mistakes which result
from representing certain facts "as if they belonged to one logical
type or category (or range of types or categories), when they actually
belong to another."[2] If this second view is correct, then many philosophical doctrines can be refuted by representing the relevant facts
in their correct categories. And, if the first position, which implies
the second, is correct, then all philosophical problems can be handled
by correctly understanding which categories are correct for representing the relevant facts.

The philosophical problem which has included the most discussion
of category mistakes is the mind-body problem. Aside from Ryle's
own attempt to refute the dualistic theory of Descartes by showing it
involves a series of category mistakes, the recent controversy about the
mind-body identity theory has included reference to category mistakes. It has, for example, been claimed that sensations and brain
processes belong to different categories so that to identify them results
in a category mistake. The question then arises of the importance of
this, whether it provides sufficient grounds to refute the identity

* Much of this paper was written while on an Andrew Mellon Postdoctoral
Fellowship at the University of Pittsburgh, 1965–66. I wish to thank the members
of that philosophy department for their many helpful comments. I owe thanks also
to John Robison of the University of Massachusetts.
[1] G. Ryle, "Categories" in *Logic and Language*, Second Series (Oxford, Basil
Blackwell, 1955), p. 80.
[2] G. Ryle, *The Concept of Mind* (London, Hutchinson & Co., 1962), p. 16.

theory, or whether, because it is "merely" a linguistic fact, it is not sufficient to refute a nonlinguistic, metaphysical theory.[3] It can be seen, consequently, that the concept of category mistake is of current philosophical interest and importance. Whether its philosophical importance is lasting is another question. Nevertheless, regardless of its philosophical status, an investigation of the concept is important if for no other reason than to clarify certain commonly accepted statements. For example, it is usually agreed that people differ from numbers in such a way that it is absurd or nonsensical to talk of people as square roots and numbers as unhappy. The absurdity in such cases seems to derive from category mistakes. But to justify that it does, we must examine category mistakes.

If we are to investigate category mistakes, we must also examine category differences because category mistakes involve terms of different categories. It would furthermore seem that we must talk about categories. However, it may not seem that there is any reason to consider what may appear to be quite different, types. Nevertheless, as we shall see, those who discuss types and those who discuss categories are trying to get at much the same thing. Furthermore we have seen above that Ryle often uses the two terms interchangeably. And, because Bertrand Russell's discussion of types predates Ryle's talk of categories, we shall begin by considering Russell's theory of types.

I. RUSSELL'S THEORY OF TYPES

What first comes to mind in a discussion of Russell's conception of type are those theories of types, both simple and ramified, which he uses to eliminate logical and semantical paradoxes. As will become clear as we proceed, neither the simple theory of types, which orders in a hierarchy individuals, properties of individuals, properties of properties of individuals, etc., nor the ramified theory, which within each type level orders propositional functions depending on the level of variables over which there is quantification, will provide us with the kind of types which can be identified with Rylean categories. However, what we can call simple types and ramified types have one thing in common with Rylean types which we can call logical types.

---

[3] The relationship of category mistakes to the mind-body identity theory has been discussed by H. Putnam, "Minds and Machines" in *Dimensions of Mind* (New York, Colliers Books, 1961), pp. 149–159; by myself in "The Identity of Mind and Body," *The Journal of Philosophy*, vol. 59 (1962), pp. 486–492; by T. Nagel, "Physicalism," *The Philosophical Review*, vol. 74 (1965), pp. 341–350; and by R. Rorty, "Mind-body Identity, Privacy, and Categories," *The Review of Metaphysics*, vol. 19 (1965), pp. 24–41.

That is, in all three cases when there is predication across types, the result is a type violation and what results is not a significant or meaningful sentence. The simple theory of types makes sentences about all properties meaningless; the ramified theory makes sentences about all properties of a certain simple type meaningless; and Ryle's theory of logical types or categories makes sentences such as "Next Saturday is in bed" meaningless. Thus all three theories of types function to rule out certain combinations of terms which otherwise might seem significant but which lead to paradoxical or absurd conclusions. Using Russell's terminology we can say that each type theory requires of certain terms "a limited range of significance." However, as we shall see, the scope of the significance ranges allowed by Ryle's theory is quite different from those allowed by either or both of Russell's theories.

This would be all there is to say about Russellean types for our purposes if Russell had not still another conception of type. Russell may have come to this third kind of type by stressing as he did that types and ranges of significance of terms are intimately related. He claimed that a type is a class of all entities which make up the range of significance of some predicate. That is, each predicate can be significantly predicated of a limited range of entities and the class of which these entities are members is a type. We can define this conception of type as follows:

Type $=$DF Class of all entities which have some predicate significantly (meaningfully) predicated of them.

It is clear that a type defined in this way need not be either a simple or a ramified type because these would place specific limits on the significance range of predicates, but this third definition of type prescribes no specific restrictions. For example, according to the simple theory, if a predicate significantly applies to individuals then it cannot be significantly applied to properties. According to the ramified theory, if a predicate is defined using quantification over predicate variables which are defined using quantification over individual variables, then the predicate cannot be significantly substituted for predicate variables which are defined using only quantification over individuals. This third definition of type, then, embodies a broader conception of type, one which can accommodate simple and ramified types as well as further restrictions within types and orders not required by the simple and ramified theories. For example, neither theory imposes any significance restrictions on the predicates predicated of individuals, but such a limitation usually is imposed by this broader theory. We can see this by considering still another of Russell's definitions of type, one which is much closer to Ryle's conception of a category. Because of this we can call this theory Russell's theory of logical types. At one point he states it as follows:

(1) The definition of a logical type is as follows: A and B are of the same logical type if, and only if, given any fact of which A is a constituent, there is a corresponding fact which has B as a constituent, which either results by substituting B for A, or is the negation of what so results.[4]

Although Russell claims this is a definition of "logical type" it is strictly speaking a definition of "A and B are of the same type." We can, however, arrive at a definition of "logical type" by using the following definition of "type":

Type $=$DF Class of all entities which are of the same type.

Thus we can define "logical type" as follows:

Logical Type $=$DF Class of all entities which are such that given any fact of which one of these entities, A, is a constituent, there is a corresponding fact which has B as a constituent, which either results by substituting B for A, or is the negation of what so results.

This is like Russell's definition of "number" in that "logical type" is defined in terms of "same logical type" so that it is the latter definition which is crucial and which requires our close scrutiny.

Black's First Objection. One objection to the previous definition, voiced by Max Black, is that this definition of "same logical type" in its present form leads to a contradiction. We can see this objection by considering what surely seems to be two facts:

(a) The fact that Russell and Socrates are of the same type.

(b) The fact that continuity and Socrates are not of the same type.

Here the second fact is the negation of what results from substituting continuity for Russell in the first fact so that by using Russell's definition we can, according to Black, derive another fact:

(c) The fact that continuity and Socrates are of the same type

But (c) contradicts (b) which, according to Black, not only shows that something is wrong with the definition but would also "seem to establish that, if there are at least three entities in the world, it is impossible that they should not all belong to the same type."[5]

---

[4] B. Russell, *Logic and Knowledge* (London, George Allen & Unwin, 1956), p. 332.

[5] M. Black, "Russell's Philosophy of Language" in *The Philosophy of Bertrand Russell* (New York, Tudor Publishing Co., 1944), p. 235.

Black's objection has two parts, but I think only the second is sound. He claims that if we hold (a) and (b) and Russell's definition (1) than we can deduce (c) which contradicts (b). And because (a) and (b) are true we must give up (1) to avoid the contradiction. However, as Black hints himself, we really need one more premiss to arrive at (c). From (a), (b), and (1) we arrive only at:

(d) The fact that Russell and continuity are of the same type

which contradicts neither (a) nor (b). Thus we also need an additional premiss such as:

(e) If two entities are each of the same type as a third, then they are of the same type.

in order to derive (c). Thus someone could maintain (a), (b), and (1) without contradiction if he gave up (e). And, although it may seem that (e) is necessarily true, so that (a), (b), and (1) entail a contradiction after all, (e) is neither necessary nor even tenable as we shall see (see Sec. IV). Consequently, we need not fear the first part of Black's objection to (1).

Nevertheless, the second part remains sound and must be handled in some way. We can see why by considering sentences of the form:

(f) The fact that X belongs to some type of other.

We can substitute any entity for X and thus by (1) can show that any two entities belong to the same type which is contrary to facts such as (b). We must, therefore, find some way to avoid the second part of Black's objection.

Black proposes that we can avoid this objection by talking of words rather than entities as being of the same or different types. Thus Russell's definition could be rewritten:

(2) 'A' and 'B' are of the same type =DF Given any fact of which A is a constituent, there is a corresponding fact which has B as a constituent, which either results by substituting B for A, or is the negation of what so results.

On this version neither part of Black's objection applies even if we accept (e). Because for (2), unlike (1), only linguistic entities can be of the same type, we must change (f) to:

(f.1) The fact that the term X belongs to some type or other.

Therefore we must substitute linguistic terms such as "Russell" and "continuity" into the fact expressed in (f.1) so that according to (2) we can infer only that the names of those terms, that is, " 'Russell' " and " 'continuity'," are of the same type. Thus Black's objection is avoided.

Black, therefore, has provided a way to avoid the objection, but it retains one bothersome feature of Russell's definition. There surely seems to be something wrong with talking about substituting entities into facts. We do not substitute continuity for the philosopher Russell nor even some other philosopher for him. What we substitute are terms that refer to philosophers and we substitute them into sentences rather than into facts. Thus if we can reformulate Russell's definition so that it refers to sentences and terms rather than to facts and constituents of facts, and so that it avoids Black's objection, then it will be preferable to either Russell's or Black's. We can state this version of Russell's definition as follows:

> (3) 'A' and 'B' are of the same logical type $=_{DF}$ Given any true sentence of which 'A' is a constituent, there is a corresponding true sentence which either results by substituting 'B' for 'A' or is the negation of what so results.

Consider Black's objection as modified for this definition. What is now relevant to the second part of Black's objection would be the sentence:

> (f.2) "The term X belongs to some type of other."

In such a sentence we would be talking about terms such as "Russell" or "continuity" so that the sentences would contain the names of those terms. Thus the constituents of such sentences are " 'Russell' " and " 'continuity'," and using (3) we could only prove that " 'continuity' " and " 'Russell' " are of the same type. Thus this formulation, although different from Black's, avoids the contradiction in a similar way. Let us, therefore, continue our discussion of Russell's theory of logical types using version (3).

It is important to notice that in both replies Black's objections have been avoided by a restatement of the definition which requires that it is linguistic expressions rather than nonlinguistic entities which are of the same or different types. This is because both restatements avoid the contradiction by making the inference from the relevant (f)-claim and the righthand side of the definition to the lefthand side (the inference that generated the contradiction) involve a jump of one semantic level. Thus this way out of the contradictions requires that the lefthand side refer to linguistic entities. However, because Russell stated his definition as about nonlinguistic entities we might try to see whether we can state a definition which at least allows for the possibility of talking about types of nonlinguistic entities and which avoids Black's objection. The obvious candidate is:

> A and B are of the same logical type $=_{DF}$ Given any true sentence of which 'A' is a constituent, there is a corresponding true sentence

which either results from substituting '*B*' for '*A*' or is the negation of what so results.

Although this definition unlike the previous one, is not limited to linguistic entities because there is no restriction on what *A* and *B* are, it does not avoid Black's objection. We can use the sentence:

(f.3) "The entity *X* belongs to some type or other"

to construct the objection because "Russell" and "continuity" could be constituents of the sentence (f.3) from which it follows that Russell and continuity are of the same type.

It might seem that this objection could be avoided if we talk of meaningful or significant sentences rather than true sentences in the definition. Such a change would at least bring the definition closer to the original general definition of a type as something related to the range of significance of linguistic expressions. This change would give us:

(4) *A* and *B* are of the same logical type =DF Given any meaningful sentence of which '*A*' is a constituent, there is a corresponding meaningful sentence which results from substituting '*B*' for '*A*'.

It can quickly be shown that (f.3) causes a problem for (4) because both "Russell" and "continuity" result in meaningful sentences when substituted into (f.3). Thus (4) does not escape the second part of Black's objection, so that it might seem that we should return to version (3) which avoids the objection. However, as we shall see, (3) is faced with another objection which can be avoided only by measures which when applied to (4) avoid Black's objection to it as well. Thus once it is amended we may be as justified using (4) to express Russell's definition about types of entities as we are using a definition about types of terms such as (3). Furthermore, there is some reason to use (4) as expressing Russell's definition of type sameness because the resulting definition of logical type is very similar to Russell's original broad definition of type already mentioned, especially if we limit the definition of logical type to subject-predicate sentences. What we get is:

Logical type =DF Class of all entities which are such that given any meaningful sentence of which the name of any one of the entities, '*A*', is a constituent, there is a corresponding meaningful sentence which results from substituting the name of some other of these entities for '*A*'.

Black's Second Objection. The second of Black's objections to Russell's definition, which is echoed by Fred Sommers and lies behind a point made by Arthur Pap, has already been intimated. The second part of Black's first objection which we saw applies to (1) and (4) but not to (2) and (3) can be shown to be merely one species of a larger problem which applies to all four definitions. Thus Black's first objection reduces to his second because only its second part is sound and, as we shall see, it is a species of the second objection. We found that by using something like (f) we could show that for (1) and (4) any two entities, or terms, are of the same type and this completely vitiates definitions (1) and (4). But the problem is not merely a problem involving (f)–claims. As interpreted by Sommers, it is that certain predicates which he calls high predicates (see Sect. IV) are significantly predicated of all entities. Examples of high predicates are "constituent of a fact," "interesting," "denoted by a word," "entity," and also "belongs to some type." Consequently if, as Russell leads us to believe, a sufficient condition for two entities, A and B, being of the same type is that one predicate can be significantly predicated of both of them or that 'A' and 'B' can be meaningfully substitutable into the same sentence, then this is truly a most serious objection not only to (1) and (4) but also to (2) and (3).

There have been two attempts to avoid this objection. One, which stems from Russell, is an attempt to avoid the objection by specifying that high predicates are systematically ambiguous.[6] Thus the sentential contexts "– – – is thought of" and "– – – is denoted by a word" are ambiguous, having different meanings when "Russell" is substituted into them from when "continuity" is substituted. Consequently, according to this way out of the objection, because high predicates are ambiguous, the sentential contexts involving them are ambiguous, and thus "Russell" cannot be substituted into the same sentential context in which "continuity" fits and the counterexample to the definition of logical type fails. Let us restate the amended version of (4) required by this reply by reference to mutual substitutability into unambiguous sentential contexts:

(5) A and B are of the same logical type =DF Given any unambiguous sentential context, 'A' can be substituted into it meaningfully if and only if 'B' can be substituted into it meaningfully.

Given this definition and the claim that high predicates including "belongs to some type" are ambiguous, we can rebut the objection because it requires high predicates. However, this is a most drastic way out because none of these high predicates seem to be ambiguous

[6] Russell, *The Philosophy of Bertrand Russell, op. cit.*, p. 691.

by any of the ordinary tests of ambiguity. What requires them to be ambiguous is merely an *ad hoc* way out of an objection. We should, therefore, look for a more plausible way to avoid the objection.

Black claims that there seems to be no way to avoid this objection "except to interpret the theory of types negatively as essentially an instrument for establishing *differences* of type."[7] We can state his suggestion as follows:

(6) *A* and *B* are of different types *if* there is at least one unambiguous sentential context into which '*A*' can be substituted meaningfully but into which '*B*' cannot be substituted meaningfully, or conversely.

This formulation clearly avoids the objection because instead of having a sufficient condition of type sameness we have only a sufficient condition of type difference. With only (6) at our disposal, however, we cannot define either type sameness nor logical type which we have been trying to do. And, although for our original purpose of elucidating the concept of category mistake a sufficient condition of type difference may be adequate, a more satisfactory result would be one that provides a definition of type difference, type sameness, and type. Let us, then, try to find a more fruitful way out of the objection.

Another Interpretation of Russell's Definition. We have been interpreting Russell's definition of type as stating that mutual substitutability into just one sentential context is a necessary and sufficient condition of type sameness and this has led to a serious objection. However, although Russell seems to interpret his definition in this way, it seems more plausible to interpret it another way. If we look back at any of the versions (1) through (5) the right-hand side always relates to *any* fact or sentence. Although "any" can be interpreted as "there is at least one" as in "Is any person home?" it usually means "every" as in "Any person can play." Indeed, it seems more plausible to interpret "any" in Russell's original definition as the universal rather than the existential quantifier and there is no other plausible interpretation for version (5) with which we are now working. On this interpretation we find that the necessary and sufficient condition of the type sameness of *A* and *B* is that '*A*' and '*B*' are meaningfully substitutable in *all* the same sentential contents. From this it follows that the necessary and sufficient condition of the type difference of *A* and *B* is that there is at least one sentential context in which '*A*' and not '*B*' is meaningfully substitutable, or the converse. This version, then, makes Black's sufficient condition of type difference

[7] Black, *op. cit.*, p. 238.

F

a necessary condition as well so that we can define logical type. Furthermore, on this interpretation high predicates present no difficulty because it is not sufficient to show that two terms are meaningfully substitutable in at least one sentential context; it must be shown that they are substitutable in *all* contexts. Consequently because on this interpretation there seems to be no reason to multiply ambiguous terms beyond necessity, no objection generated by high predicates, and no problem about defining logical type, we should prefer this interpretation to other versions of Russell's definition and to Black's negative reformulation.

Smart's Objection to Definition (5). Although version (5) of Russell's definition of type is the most preferable of those we have examined so far, it also faces objections. The first is adapted from the objection J. J. C. Smart raises to Ryle's theory of logical type which we shall examine later.[8] Smart claims that although the sentence "The seat of the chair is hard" is meaningful, it surely seems that "The seat of the bed is hard" makes no sense at all. Consequently, because "chair" and "bed" do not both go significantly into one sentential context, we can conclude using version (5) that chairs and beds are of different logical types. But, paraphrasing Smart, if pieces of furniture are not of the same logical type, then we might well ask what is. In other words, Smart's example seems to show that version (5) prescribes a sufficient condition of type difference which separates into different logical types entities which surely seem to belong to the same type. This, then, is an objection to Black's negative reformulation of Russell's definition. We can, of course, avoid it by considering universal substitutability merely a sufficient condition of type sameness, but we cannot rest content merely with that because we need a sufficient condition of type difference to help us with category mistakes. We should, then, continue the search for a satisfactory necessary and sufficient condition of type sameness.

Another objection to version (5) is that even if it will do as a definition of type sameness, it will not be a satisfactory criterion of type sameness. That is, although version (5) provides a sufficient condition of type sameness, a criterion of type is not merely a sufficient condition. It should be a sufficient condition which can be used to decide that different entities, whether nonlinguistic or linguistic, are of the same type. However, the sufficient condition of type sameness provided by version (5) cannot be met unless all sentential contexts have been investigated which is at best too unwieldy to help us decide.

[8] J. J. C. Smart, "A Note on Categories," *The British Journal for the Philosophy of Science*, vol. 4 (1953–1954), pp. 227–228.

What is required for a criterion is something like Black's existential interpretation of the sufficient condition which can avoid the objections to Black's interpretation. We should, therefore, continue our search for a satisfactory criterion of type sameness.

II. Pap's Definition of Type

Arthur Pap, who rejects the existential version of Russell's definition of type sameness for several reasons, including one like Black's objection, proposes a definition of type which he thinks avoids the troubles facing a definition in terms of type sameness. He states it as follows:

> *A type is a class such that there are families of predicates which can be significantly, i.e., correctly or falsely, ascribed to all and only members of it.* A predicate family is a set of predicates such that one and only one member of it must be true of anything of which some member of the set is true or false.[9]

By incorporating the definition of "predicate family" into the definition we get the following:

Type $=$DF Class of all entities for which there is a set of predicates such that:

- (a) each predicate of the set can be significantly ascribed to all and only members of the set, and
- (b) one and only one predicate of the set must be true of any entity of which some predicate of the set can be significantly ascribed.

What we have is rather cumbersome. However, we can simplify it considerably by taking as a predicate family one predicate and its complement so that condition (b) is obviated. For example, if we take P and non-P as the members of a predicate family which are significantly ascribable to certain entities as required by (a), then it follows that one and only one of the two predicates must be true of the entities. Furthermore, because non-P can be significantly ascribed to an entity just in case P can, we need mention only P in the definition. What we have is:

Type $=$DF Class of all entities for which there is a predicate, P, which can be significantly ascribed to all and only members of the class.

When, however, we look at this simplified version of Pap's definition we can see that it is equivalent to the definition of "logical type"

[9] A. Pap, "Types and Meaninglessness," *Mind*, vol. 69 (1960), p. 48.

we would get if we defined it in terms of the existential interpretation of version (4) of Russell's definition of type sameness, and limited the contexts to subject-predicate sentences. It would seem, then, that the problem which we saw generated by high predicates would arise all over again. But this is not so, because, as Pap sees, his definition implies nothing about the relationship between sameness and difference of type. Pap is free to define sameness and difference of type as he wishes. What he does is to admit that types need not be mutually exclusive. Indeed one type can even be a subclass of another. He gives an example of such types when he says,

> Physical objects constitute a type because weight predicates and predicates of location in physical space are restricted to physical objects. But there are also predicate families which are restricted to animals: if it is meaningless to ascribe a weight or a location in physical space to a thought, or to a number, it is equally meaningless to say of a stone that it drinks milk or that it expects food, etc.[10]

According to Pap, therefore, entities "which belong to a common type may belong to different types."[11] What Pap has done is reject the implication:

If entities are of a same type, then they are not of different types, which allows him to avoid the high predicate objection and also Smart's objection. For example, although on Pap's definition both continuity and Socrates turn out to be of a same type, we cannot infer from this the seemingly false conclusion that they are not of different types. And, although Pap might agree with Smart that his definition requires beds and chairs to be of different types, it does not follow from this that they do not have the type furniture in common.

Comparison of Russell's Definition and Pap's Definition. Pap has found a definition of type which avoids the objections we have discussed. It appears that he thought he had done this by proposing a definition different from the existential version of Russell's definition, but what he actually did was point out that the problems for Russell's definition of type sameness arise only if an inference is made which requires the implication stated above. If we reject that implication, then we can accept the existential version in spite of Black's claim that we can save it only by a negative reformulation. It seems clear that if rejecting the implication has no objectionable consequences, then we should prefer Pap's theory of types to those we have already examined.

[10] *Ibid.*, p. 50.
[11] *Ibid.*, pp. 42–43.

We can further emphasize the difference between Russell's theory of types and Pap's reformulation by interpreting the difference as a difference in the definition of type difference. As we have seen, both men can use the same definition of type, and, furthermore, Pap could agree to the existential interpretation of Russell's definition of type sameness, namely:

A is of the same type as *B* =DF There is an unambiguous sentential context such that both '*A*' and '*B*' can be substituted into it meaningfully.

Where they differ is that Russell seems to interpret type difference so that *A* and *B* are of different types if and only if they are not of the same type, or in other words on the existential interpretation of type sameness:

A and *B* are of different types =DF No unambiguous sentential context is such that both '*A*' and '*B*' can be substituted into it meaningfully.

Pap, however, seems to have an existential interpretation of type difference, namely,

A and *B* are of different types =DF There is an unambiguous sentential context such that '*A*' or '*B*' but not both can be substituted into it meaningfully.

It is clear that for Pap, *A* and *B* can be of the same type and also of different types contrary to Russell's theory. The question this brings up is whether this difference about type difference is important.

One consequence of Pap's definition is that there is no guarantee of the type and order strata to which Russell's simple and ramified theories lead. That is, if we assume, as both men would, that each property of something is of a simple type different from each individual to which it is ascribable, then, for example, each property of an individual is of a different simple type from each individual to which it is ascribable. And if we also make the assumption that each property of an individual is ascribable to each individual, then on Russell's theory we get the beginning of the hierarchy of Russell's simple theory of types. But given these two assumptions, we do not get the hierarchy on Pap's theory because although it follows from the assumptions that each property of an individual and each individual are of different types, it does not also follow, as it does for Russell, that they have no types in common. It might be thought that this is an important difference between the two theories because Pap's theory does not have Russell's guarantee against paradoxes. However, although on Pap's theory a hierarchical guarantee is missing given the addition of only these two assumptions, it does not follow that there is no way Pap's theory can be supplemented to avoid the paradoxes. Indeed the underlying assumption common to both theories, that each property is of a different type from that to which it is ascribable, is all that is needed to avoid the "simple" paradoxes. Thus it is not meaningful to say that the property of being impredicable is impredicable because, according to both theories, if it is meaningful, then the property of being impredicable is ascribable to itself from which it follows that the property is of a different type from itself which is false on either interpretation of type difference.

An Objection to Pap's Definition. We have found that there are no objections to Pap's theory which are the result of an incapacity to avoid paradoxes. There is, however, another reason we might prefer a different kind of theory. It might be claimed that Russell's way of avoiding the paradoxes seems to be somewhat *ad hoc,* devised as it is merely to avoid paradoxes. However, it is not completely *ad hoc* because there are consequences of Russell's theory which go well beyond the mere avoidance of paradoxes. That is, not only does Russell's theory allow us to avoid paradoxes, it also has consequences for significance and ambiguity which are independent of the paradoxes. Although some of these consequences are undesirable, taken altogether they do provide us with a way to test the theory and perhaps to discover certain nonsignificant sentences which will have important philosophical as well as nonphilosophical consequences. This is not so for Pap's theory. For example, we cannot define a type or category mistake as the use of a sentence which predicates a predicate, appropriate to one logical type, of an entity that belongs to a different logical type, and then go on to infer, as we might want, that the sentence involves a conceptual or semantical mistake and is therefore meaningless. This is because given Pap's definition of type difference we can infer at most that there is one predicate which results in a meaningless sentence. Many predicates would be appropriate to many different types such as the predicates appropriate to stones and also to animals, two entities of different types. Here, then, is an important point at which Pap diverges from Russell and, as we shall see, from Ryle as well. But this is not the only important inference we cannot draw given Pap's definition of type difference. There really is nothing we can infer from a case of type difference except what we use to establish type differences: that there is at least one predicate which is not predicable of the entities in question. Pap's theory, then is completely *ad hoc* for it functions only to avoid paradoxes, but cannot be justified or rejected on any independent grounds. Indeed, his version of the simple theory of types comes down to the statement that no property is ascribable to itself. This avoids the paradox but does so by fiat instead of by a conceptually testable theory.

The Problem of High Predicates Again. Although this objection to Pap's theory by no means demolishes it, it is sufficient, I think, to set us looking for a theory which has more semantical explanatory and predicative power than Pap's, but which can avoid the objection to Russell's theory. However, in moving away from the discussion of Pap's theory we should not overlook the important point brought out by the discussion that we have not avoided the total force of the objection from high predicates by adopting the universal definition of type. As we have just seen, on Russell's theory and for our purposes the implication:

If *A* and *B* are of different types, then no predicate is significantly ascribable to both *A* and *B*.

seems to be of central importance. But, as we have also seen, if high predicates are univocal, this implication is obviously false, so that if we wish to defend the implication, we seem forced to agree with Russell after all that they are ambiguous. Pap rejects the implication and avoids excessive ambiguity, but does so in such a way that type differences are of no importance for our purposes. Russell saves the implication but only by forcing "thought of," "denoted by," and other high predicates into an unnatural ambiguity. We should try to avoid both of these alternatives and the only way to do this is to modify the implication so that it has the kind of consequences we require, but avoids excessive ambiguity. The most promising way to do this, which as we shall see is the way taken by Sommers, is to make an explicit exception of high predicates in the implication. Thus:

For any predicate, *P*, if *A* and *B* are of different types and *P* is not a high predicate, then *P* is not significantly ascribable to both *A* and *B*.

This is something like what Pap seems to be implying when he says that "type predicates are significantly applicable to everything,"[12] because type predicates are one kind of high predicates. This modification does not take us very far, however, because we are faced with the task of providing some criterion for high predicates. If we can do

---

[12] *Ibid.*, p. 48.

this we can return to a modified version of the existential definition of type sameness and thereby avoid the unwieldy universal definition. However, before we pursue this further, let us turn to an examination of Ryle's theory of types or categories because we are particularly interested in category mistakes as discussed by Ryle and we do not want to stray too far away from what Ryle means. This might happen, for example, if we pursued Russell's theory along the path suggested by Pap. Let us examine Ryle's theory and then see how it compares with Russell's as we now understand it.

III. RYLE AND CATEGORIES

Ryle says that "the logical type or category to which a concept belongs is the set of ways in which it is logically legitimate to operate with it."[13] However, such a quick characterization is of little help in arriving at a final definition. For one thing, a category is not a set of ways of operating with a concept. It would be more accurate to say that it is a set of all the sentential contexts in which the term can be legitimately used. Another interpretation, closer to the conception we worked with in the discussion of Russellian types, is that a category is a set of all terms which can be legitimately used in the same sentential contexts. Although Ryle does not say anything explicitly about categories more helpful than this, he has made a quite definite statement about category differences, which, of course, is what is essential to category mistakes. In "Categories" he says:

> Two proposition-factors are of different categories or types, if there are sentence-frames such that when the expressions for those factors are imported as alternative complements to the same gap-signs, the resultant sentences are significant in the one case and absurd in the other.[14]

If we let 'A' and 'B' stand for what Ryle means by proposition factors and add the requirement of unambiguity, we can translate this quotation as:

(7) 'A' and 'B' are of different categories or types, if there is at least one unambiguous sentential context into which 'A' can be substituted meaningfully, but into which 'B' cannot be substituted meaningfully, or conversely.

Interpreted this way, Ryle's statement about category differences is like (6), which was our final version of Black's suggestion about Russell's definition, with the one exception that in (7) the entities

---

[13] G. Ryle, *The Concept of Mind*, *op. cit.*, p. 8.
[14] G. Ryle, "Categories," *op. cit.*, pp. 77–78.

which are of different types must be linguistic while in (6) the only requirement is that they are one semantic level below the linguistic entities mentioned on the right-hand side. Nevertheless, in order not to blur over the differences between Russellian types and Rylean categories, we should note two things: that whereas Russell's original formulation, (1), considered nonlinguistic entities and facts, Ryle's considers linguistic terms and sentences; and that although in our final formulation of Russell's definition we found it better to talk of sentences rather than facts, there still remains the nonlinguistic entity —linguistic term difference. This may well be an important difference because whereas Russell's definition as we revised it requires an inference from a premiss about sentences to a conclusion about entities, Ryle's requires merely an intralinguistic inference. Thus someone might accept Ryle's definition but reject Russell's because, for example, he rejects the implication:

If 'A' and 'B' are of different types, then A and B are of different types.

on purely ontological grounds.[15]

A Rylean Definition of Type. Another difference between Russell's and Ryle's treatment of type difference is that Russell provides a necessary and sufficient condition of type sameness and therefore of type difference, while Ryle states merely a sufficient condition of type difference and thus only a necessary condition of type sameness. Ryle has done enough for someone interested only in establishing category mistakes, but it surely would be preferable if an "if and only if" definition which created no additional problems could be found. What is needed is in addition to (7) is:

(8) If 'A' and 'B' are of different categories or types, then there is at least one unambiguous sentential context into which 'A' can be substituted meaningfully, but into which 'B' cannot be substituted meaningfully, or conversely.

It might be thought that Ryle rejects (8) because he claims that the converse of what we have interpreted as (7) is false.[16] However although (8) is the converse of (7) it is not equivalent to what Ryle calls the converse, namely:

[15] A mind-body identity theorist, for example, might claim that "sensation" and "brain process" belong to different logical categories, but also want to deny that sensations and brain processes belong to different categories because sensations are identical with brain processes.

[16] G. Ryle, "Categories," *op. cit.*, p. 78.

(9) If there is *at least one* unambiguous sentential context into which both '*A*' and '*B*' can be substituted meaningfully, then '*A*' and '*B*' are of the *same* type.

What (7) and (8) give us is:

(10) '*A*' and '*B*' are of the *same* type =DF Give *any* unambiguous sentential context, '*A*' can be substituted into it meaningfully if and only if '*B*' can be substituted into it meaningfully.

Thus although Ryle is right in rejecting (9) with its existential formulation of type sameness, this provides no reason to reject (8) which is equivalent to a universal formulation. Thus if (8) is acceptable we can accept (10) as a Rylean definition of type sameness and can as a consequence define "category" in the same way "type" was defined by Russell.

The only situation in which we would find reason to reject (8) would be one in which '*A*' and '*B*' are meaningful in all the same sentential contexts but belong to different categories. But because there would be absolutely no reason to claim they belong to different categories if there was not one context in which one was meaningful but the other was not, we can eliminate this situation. Thus we can accept (8) and conjoin it with (7) to give the Rylean definition of type sameness expressed in (10). This turns out to be the Russellian definition (5) with the one exception that (10) requires that we talk only of linguistic expressions being of the same type. And, with a different exception, (10) is equivalent to definition (3) with the addition of the unambiguity amendment. Definition (3) concerns true sentences while (10) considers only meaningful sentences. There is one way that this difference is important. If we use definition (3), then because we must work with true sentences we must have some grounds for claiming that the sentences we work with are true if we are to justify the conclusion we reach about the categories of '*A*' and '*B*'. For (10) we need only have reason to think that the sentences are meaningful so that we can be justified in applying (10) when we are not justified in using (3), but the converse is false. Consequently (10) is easier to use and, *ceteris paribus*, we should use it instead of (3). And, indeed, there is no difference in the conclusions we reach about the type sameness or difference of '*A*' and '*B*' because it is irrelevant for the purpose of the definition whether the sentence we pick with '*A*' or its denial is true. Whatever we can conclude from substituting '*B*' for '*A*' in a sentence would also be concluded by substituting it into the denial of that sentence regardless of which sentence is true. We only need to know that for any sentence using

'*A*', it has truth-value if and only if the corresponding sentence using '*B*' has truth-value. Consequently because (10) differs from (3) and (5) in unobjectionable ways and thus expresses an unobjectionable version of Russell's definition, and because it expresses Ryle's claim with an unobjectionable clause added, we shall use (10) in any future discussion of the views of Russell and Ryle.

Objections to Definition (10). Having seen that (10) is much like (3) and also (5), it is not surprising that objections to them also apply to (10). In fact, one of the objections, Smart's, was originally raised against Ryle's claim about type difference. His objection applies to (7) and thus to (10). Smart claims that "chair" goes significantly into "The seat of the – – – is hard" but "bed" does not, so that by (7) we get the seemingly false conclusion that "chair" and "bed" belong to different categories. And if, as discussed above, we can conclude from this that only high predicates are significantly ascribable to both "chair" and "bed" then we must also conclude that predicates like "heavy," "red," "large," and "wooden" are either high predicates or ambiguous which is surely unsatisfactory.

Definition (10), like (5), makes meaningful substitutability into all sentential contexts a necessary and sufficient condition of type sameness, so that it avoids the high predicate objection. It is, however, open to the objections that it provides a most unwieldy criterion of type sameness and that it does not help with the problem of how to determine for any particular predicate whether or not it is significantly ascribable to entities of different types. Furthermore, we have just seen the problem generated by Smart's objection as it applies to (7) and therefore to (10). There is also a problem we have not discussed yet, i.e., the problem of finding a test for sentential meaningfulness and meaninglessness which can be used with a definition such as (10) to arrive at a conclusion about type differences. Consequently although (10) faces no problems not faced by versions (3) and (5) of the Russellian definition, and is preferable to (3) because it does not require that we know the truth-value of sentences, and is a less vulnerable claim than (5) because it avoids inferences from language to entities, it is still not a definition with which we can rest content. We must try to handle the above problems.

IV. Sommers' Criterion of Type Sameness

We have found no way to state a sufficient condition of type sameness which both avoids the high predicate objection as the universal version does, and is a useable criterion as the existential version is. In two recent articles Fred Sommers has proposed such a criterion by concentrating upon the high predicate problem. Sommers, in effect, criticizes the criteria of both Russell and Ryle because they overlook this problem and then he proposed an amendment to eliminate the problem. What in his proposal is central for our purposes is that it uses an existential criterion which although it allows us to infer the type sameness of two predicates from their meaningful substitution into one sentential context, requires that any such context itself contains no predicate which are higher than both the two predicates being tested. Thus Sommers' amendment, in effect, rules out the use of sentential contexts containing high predicates and thus avoids the high predicate objection. What is essential, then, is that he define what it is for one predicate to be higher than the other. What he actually does is define what it is for one predicate to be higher than two others.

High Predicates and a Criterion of Type Sameness. We can state Sommer's definition as:

A predicate 'A' is higher than the predicates 'B' and 'C'=DF A general sentence (such as "All A is B") using 'A' and 'B' is meaningful and a general sentence using 'A' and 'C' is meaningful, but a general sentence using 'B' and 'C' is not meaningful.

Using Sommers' terminology, where he drops the single quotes and uses $U(AB)$ to mean that a general sentence with predicates 'A' and 'B' is meaningful and $N(AB)$ to mean that it is not meaningful, we can state his definition as:

A is a higher predicate than B and than C =DF $U(AB)\&U(AC)$ $\&N(BC)$.[17]

Although Sommers uses this concept in his criterion, we have seen that all he needs is a criterion that requires that the predicate of the sentential context C is not higher than one of the predicates being tested, either A or B. This would guarantee that C is not a high predicate. We can achieve this by using a fourth predicate D which is meaningful with A or B but not with C. Thus we want $U(AD)$ or $U(BD)$ but $N(CD)$. By conjoining this with the basic requirement of the existential criterion that A and B are both meaningful with a third predicate C, and by assuming the nonambiguity amendment, as we shall from here on, we get using Sommers' terminology:

[17] Cf. F. Sommers, "The Ordinary Language Tree," *Mind*, vol. 68 (1959), pp. 172–173.

(11) If $\{\{[U(AD) \text{ v } U(BD)] \& N(CD)\} \& [U(AC) \& U(BC)]\}$ then $S(AB)$, i.e., A and B are of the same logical category.[18]

It should be noted that (11) provides only a sufficient condition of type sameness. It might be thought that just as we found the converse of (7) to be unobjectionable so that we could arrive at the "if and only if" definition (10), so also we could use the converse of (11). However, the converse of (11) implies:

If $S(AB)$ then $N(CD)$

which states that two terms being of the same type implies that there are two other terms of different types. This is surely dubious and is clearly false for any language with only two predicates or for any language with all its terms of the same type as is at least possible. Thus we should not use the converse of (11). This is not troublesome, however, if we can continue to use (10) as a definition, for if so, we need in addition only a sufficient condition of type sameness which is useable and which avoids the high predicate objection.

We can see how (11) avoids this objection by letting $A=$person, $B=$number, and $C=$thought of. Consequently we get $U(AC)$ and $U(BC)$ which on the original existential definition would have led us to the false conclusion that "person" and "number" are of the same logical category. However, to reach this conclusion on Sommers criterion we also need a D such that:

$[U(AD) \text{ v } U(BD)] \& N(CD)$

but there is no D with which "thought of" cannot be joined significantly so the inference is invalid. This is also true of the other high predicates such as "interesting," "denoted by a word," "an entity," "of same type," and others. Consequently because Sommers' criterion is existential and avoids the high predicate objection it may be what we need to establish type sameness. It can be adapted to result in a criterion for type difference, but there is a question of whether the existential criterion of type difference, (7), requires any amendment. Sommers thinks that it does, however, because (7) which he would state as:

$[U(AC) \& N(BC)] \supset D(AB)$, i.e., A and B are of different categories

is, he claims, equivalent to:

$[U(AC) \& U(AB)] \supset S(BC)$

and this is falsified by the high predicate examples. These two sentences are equivalent, however, only if $D(AB)$ implies $N(AB)$ which

[18] *Ibid.*, p. 173.

is not obvious. In fact if we accept (7), that implication is false. Let A=entity, B=number, and C=heavy, so that by (7) we get D (entity, number). But it surely is true that U (entity, number) so that the implication required for Sommers' equivalence is false. Thus (7) can escape Sommers attack. However, we should not hold (7) with (11) because taken together they produce results which are surely unsatisfactory. We have found that (7) gives us D(entity, number), and we can show that (11) gives us S(entity, number) by letting A=entity, B=number, C=sum of two numbers and D=heavy. It seems we should then give up either (7) or (11), but which one?

The Rejection of Criterion (7) *and a New Definition of Type Difference.* It would seem that (7) should be discarded because numbers are entities so that "number" and "entity" should be construed as being in the same logical category. But stones are also entities so that "stone" should be put in the same category as "entity" and consequently, it would seem, as "number." But if any two terms belong in different categories it is "stone" and "number." We can avoid this problem by prohibiting the inference from $S(AC)$ and $S(AB)$ to $S(BC)$, that is, denying statement (e):

> If two entities are each of the same type as a third, then they are of the same type.

which we saw was essential to the first part of Black's objection to Russell's definition (see Sect. I). This, in effect, is what Sommers does because he claims that $S(XY)=U(XY)$ and we know that $U(AC)$ and $U(BC)$ do not imply $U(AB)$. With this he also claims that $D(XY)=N(XY)$ which we have seen is false if we use (7) because it is then false that $D(XY)$ implies $N(XY)$. This, I think, provides the best reason for rejecting (7). There is no reason to establish $D(AB)$ unless we can infer from this $N(AB)$ and thus establish a method to rule out sentences using both A and B as illegitimate. If the inference from $D(AB)$ to $N(AB)$ is invalid, then there is no value in establishing that two terms are of different categories. Therefore because the inference is invalid if we use (7) we should either amend (7) or give it up altogether.

The problem we must eliminate is that (7) requires us to put two terms into different categories when one, A, is so much higher than the other, B, that A can be used significantly with lower terms not significantly useable with B. This is the problem involved with the three terms "entity," "number," and "stone." As stated (7) prohibits only one of the terms, either A or B, from being higher than the other. Thus if we write (7) using Sommers' terminology except for variables instead of C and D in order to emphasize the existential character of (7), we get:

(7a) $\{(\exists X)[U(AX) \& N(BX)] \lor (\exists Y)[U(BY) \& N(AY)]\} \supset D(AB)$.

Criterion (7a) tells us that if we can find one term that goes meaningfully with A but not with B, or goes meaningfully with B but not with A, then $D(AB)$. According to (7a), then, we can establish $D(AB)$ by verifying either:

(12) $(\exists X)[U(AX) \& N(BX)]$

which guarantees that B is not higher than A or:

(13) $(\exists Y)[U(BY) \& N(AY)]$

which guarantees that A is not higher than B. But it is not enough to guarantee that just one term is not higher than the other, because that is compatible with the other being a high predicate. We can remedy this defect by requiring that neither term be higher than the other. We need, then, the conjunction of (12) and (13) in the antecedent of the criterion rather than the disjunction. Thus:

(14) $\{(\exists X)[U(AX) \& N(BX)] \& (\exists Y)[U(BY) \& N(AY)]\} \supset D(AB)$[19]

As before we have the problem of determining whether the converse of (14) is acceptable so that we can arrive at an "if and only if" definition. In this case the converse seems innocuous as can be seen by realizing that it is equivalent to:

(15) $\{(X)[U(AX) \supset U(BX)] \lor (Y)[U(BY) \supset U(AY)]\} \supset S(AB)$

This claims that if either A or B is significant with all the terms the other is, then the two are of the same category. This requires that each high predicate belongs to every category which is also one unobjectionable consequence of (11). Also (15), like (11), allows terms like "object" and "event" which strictly speaking are not high predicates, because not significant with everything, to be significant with terms not significant with each other. This is an important consequence because it requires that we either give up or further amend the previously amended implication:

> For any predicate, P, if A and B are of different types and P is not a high predicate, then P is not significantly ascribable to both A and B.

to account for nonhigh predicates such as "object" and "event." However, because a decision on this point is not necessary for establishing criteria of category difference and sameness, I shall pursue it no further here. For now let us accept (15) as unobjectionable so we arrive at the definition:

[19] Cf. F. Sommers, "Types and Ontology," *The Philosophical Review*, vol. 72 (1963), p. 358, for a derivation of an equivalent criterion.

(16) $D(AB)=$ DF. $(\exists X)(\exists Y)[U(AX)$ & $N(BX)$ & $U(BY)$ & $N(AY)]$

A Problem for Criterion (11). Although (15) provides a sufficient condition for type sameness, it is, like (8), a universal condition which is unwieldy to use. Thus it seems we should use (11) as a criterion of type sameness instead. However, although (11) seems to be an easily useable criterion because we need only find two terms, C and D, that meet its requirements, it does not seem that for every pair of terms, A and B, there is such a pair, C and D. Consider the two terms "dog" and "cat." They seem to be of the same category but I do not see how to show this using (11). Consider the following quantified version of (11):

(11a) $(\exists X)(\exists Y)\{[U(AX) \vee U(BX)]$ & $N(XY)$ & $[U(AY)$ & $U(BY)]\}$ $\supset S(AB).$

We need an X and Y such that $U(\text{dog}, X)$, $N(XY)$, $U(\text{dog}, Y)$ and $U(\text{cat}, Y)$; but I cannot find two terms that go with "dog" and "cat" but not with each other. Thus it seems that although where (11) can be applied it can be used as a criterion, it does not apply in all cases. Indeed it seems applicable only where one of the terms is considerably higher than the other. It may be, then, we shall have to fall back on (15) and verify its universally quantified antecedent inductively. This is not a completely satisfactory solution, but we shall have to rest content with it, at least in this paper. I want to concentrate here upon category difference now that we have reached a criterion for that which is useable, and, if we can handle the Smart problem, unobjectionably.

Smart's Objection Applied to Definition (16). The Smart problem is that if we accept (7) as the criterion for type difference, then we must conclude that "chair" and "bed" are of different categories because $U(\text{chair, hard seat})$ and $N(\text{bed, hard seat})$. But surely these two terms belong in the same category because both are pieces of furniture. This objection would seem also to apply to (14) and therefore (16) if we take $A=$chair, $B=$bed, $X=$hard seat, and $Y=$box springs. The only way I can find to handle this objection is to deny $N(BX)$ or $N(AY)$ so the conditions of (14) are not met. This may seem strange but one intuitive way to judge some cases of type sameness is by wondering whether a normal perceiver could perceive something which is B and X, or A and Y. If he might perceive such a thing, no matter how odd, then $U(BX)$ and $U(AY)$. It surely is possible to see a bed with a seat, and a chair made partly from a box spring. However, someone might reconstruct the objection using $A=$chair, $B=$rug, $X=$legs, and $Y=1/8$ inch thick. My intuition here is that we should conclude that $D(AB)$ even though someone might claim they are both furniture. Rugs, are, however, quite unlike chairs, enough to belong in a different category. Thus we may be able to avoid the Smart objection and accept definition (16).

V. Conclusion

I have suggested the Smart objection seems avoidable and have relied on my intuition in doing. But my intuitions about "chair" and "rug" are not so clear as those about "number" and "heavy" for example. It may seem that relying on intuitions is risky as these examples show. This is true, but ultimately we must rest on our intuitions both in using criteria of category sameness and difference, such as definition (16), to decide problematic cases, and in testing the criteria themselves by trying to find counter-examples to them. For both purposes we must rely on unproblematic cases. Such cases, where not previously established by some criterion, are only those in which our intuitions are clear.

We have not found a clear counterexample to definition (16). We have, then, reason to think it is satisfactory. This completes our discussion, except for one point. Throughout the paper there has arisen the question of whether or not we could find a principle warranting an inference from the fact that two terms are of different categories to a conclusion about whether predicates significant with one are not significant with the other. We found first that high predicates such as "interesting" and "thought of" and then that other "relatively high" predicates such as "event" and "object" are significant with terms of different categories. Because of this we found no way to state a justifiable principle. Thus, given what we have developed in this paper, the most we can infer from the fact that two terms are of different categories is that those two terms result in a category mistake when used together. Therefore unless we adopt a theory of language strata such as Russell's simple theory of types, or unless we find a suitable amendment to the principle stated (at end of Sect. II) we shall have to decide about each case of purported category mistake by direct application of the criterion. This is, perhaps, unwieldy, but it may be the best we can do, because it is not clear that there is good reason to adopt a theory of language strata, or that the principle can be amended with a suitable inference restriction. Nevertheless, unwieldy or not, if the criterion is workable, as it seems, then there is available the core of a satisfactory method for determining category mistakes. What remains is primarily a matter of refinement.

University of Pennsylvania
G

IV

A Theory of Conditionals

ROBERT C. STALNAKER*

I. Introduction

A conditional sentence expresses a proposition which is a function of two other propositions, yet not one which is a *truth* function of those propositions. I may know the truth values of "Willie Mays played in the American League" and "Willie Mays hit four hundred" without knowing whether or not Mays would have hit four hundred if he had played in the American League. This fact has tended to puzzle, displease, or delight philosophers, and many have felt that it is a fact that calls for some comment or explanation. It has given rise to a number of philosophical problems; I shall discuss three of these.

My principal concern will be with what has been called the *logical problem of conditionals*, a problem that frequently is ignored or dismissed by writers on conditionals and counterfactuals. This is the task of describing the formal properties of the *conditional function*: a function, usually represented in English by the words "if . . . then," taking ordered pairs of propositions into propositions. I shall explain informally and defend a solution, presented more rigorously elsewhere, to this problem.[1]

The second issue—the one that has dominated recent discussions of contrary-to-fact conditionals—is the *pragmatic problem of counterfactuals*. This problem derives from the belief, which I share with most philosophers writing about this topic, that the formal properties of the conditional function, together with all of the *facts*, may not be sufficient for determining the truth value of a counterfactual; that is,

* I want to express appreciation to my colleague, Professor R. H. Thomason, for his collaboration in the formal development of the theory expounded in this paper, and for his helpful comments on its exposition and defense.

The preparation of this paper was supported in part by a National Science Foundation grant, GS–1567.

[1] R. C. Stalnaker and R. H. Thomason, "A Semantic Analysis of Conditional Logic" (forthcoming). In this paper, the formal system, C2, is proved sound and semantically complete with respect to the interpretation sketched in the present paper. That is, it is shown that a formula is a consequence of a class of formulas if and only if it is derivable from the class in the formal system, C2.

different truth valuations of conditional statements may be consistent with a single valuation of all nonconditional statements. The task set by the problem is to find and defend criteria for choosing among these different valuations.

This problem is different from the first issue because these criteria are pragmatic, and not semantic. The distinction between semantic and pragmatic criteria, however, depends on the construction of a semantic theory. The semantic theory that I shall defend will thus help to clarify the second problem by charting the boundary between the semantic and pragmatic components of the concept. The question of this boundary line is precisely what Rescher, for example, avoids by couching his whole discussion in terms of conditions for belief, or justified belief, rather than truth conditions. Conditions for justified belief are pragmatic for any concept. [2]

The third issue is an epistemological problem that has bothered empiricist philosophers. It is based on the fact that many counterfactuals seem to be synthetic, and contingent, statements about unrealized possibilities. But contingent statements must be capable of confirmation by empirical evidence, and the investigator can gather evidence only in the actual world. How are conditionals which are both empirical and contrary-to-fact possible at all? How do we learn about possible worlds, and where are the facts (or counterfacts) which make counterfactuals true? Such questions have led philosophers to try to analyze the conditional in non-conditional terms [3]—to show that conditionals merely appear to be about unrealized possibilities. My approach, however, will be to accept the appearance as reality, and to argue that one can sometimes have evidence about nonactual situations.

In Sects. II and III of this paper, I shall present and defend a theory of conditionals which has two parts: a formal system with a primitive conditional connective, and a semantical apparatus which provides general truth conditions for statements involving that connective. In Sects. IV, V and VI, I shall discuss in a general way the relation of the theory to the three problems outlined above.

---

[2] N. Rescher, *Hypothetical Reasoning* (Amsterdam, 1964).

[3] Cf. R. Chisholm, "The Contrary-to-fact Conditional," *Mind*, vol. 55 (1946), pp. 289–307, reprinted in *Readings in Philosophical Analysis*, ed. by H. Feigl and W. Sellars (New York, 1949), pp. 482–497. The problem is sometimes posed (as it is here) as the task of analyzing the *subjunctive* conditional into an indicative statement, but I think it is a mistake to base very much on the distinction of mood. As far as I can tell, the mood tends to indicate something about the attitude of the speaker, but in no way effects the propositional content of the statement.

II. THE INTERPRETATION

Eventually, I want to defend a hypothesis about the truth conditions for statements having conditional form, but I shall begin by asking a more practical question: how does one evaluate a conditional statement? How does one decide whether or not he believes it to be true? An answer to this question will not be a set of truth conditions, but it will serve as a heuristic aid in the search for such a set.

To make the question more concrete, consider the following situation: you are faced with a true-false political opinion survey. The statement is, "If the Chinese enter the Vietnam conflict, the United States will use nuclear weapons." How do you deliberate in choosing your response? What considerations of a logical sort are relevant? I shall first discuss two familiar answers to this question, and then defend a third answer which avoids some of the weaknesses of the first two.

The first answer is based on the simplest account of the conditional, the truth functional analysis. According to this account, you should reason as follows in responding to the true-false quiz: you ask yourself, first, will the Chinese enter the conflict? and second, will the United States use nuclear weapons? If the answer to the first question is no, *or* if the answer to the second is yes, then you should place your *X* in the "true" box. But this account is unacceptable since the following piece of reasoning is an obvious *non sequitur*: "I firmly believe that the Chinese will stay out of the conflict; *therefore* I believe that the statement is true." The falsity of the antecedent is never sufficient reason to affirm a conditional, even an indicative conditional.

A second answer is suggested by the shortcomings of the truth-functional account. The material implication analysis fails, critics have said, because it leaves out the idea of *connection* which is implicit in an if-then statement. According to this line of thought, a conditional is to be understood as a statement which affirms that some sort of logical or casual connection holds between the antecedent and the consequent. In responding to the true-false quiz, then, you should look, not at the truth values of the two clauses, but at the relation between the propositions expressed by them. If the "connection" holds, you check the "true" box. If not, you answer "false."

If the second hypothesis were accepted, then we would face the task of clarifying the idea of "connection," but there are counter-examples even with this notion left as obscure as it is. Consider the following case: you firmly believe that the use of nuclear weapons by the United States in this war is inevitable because of the arrogance of power, the bellicosity of our president, rising pressure from congressional hawks, or other *domestic* causes. You have no opinion about future Chinese actions, but you do not think they will make much difference one way or another to nuclear escalation. Clearly, you believe the opinion survey statement to be true even though you believe the antecedent and consequent to be logically and casually independent of each other. It seems that the presence of a "connection" is not a necessary condition for the truth of an if-then statement.

The third answer that I shall consider is based on a suggestion made some time ago by F. P. Ramsey.[4] Consider first the case where you have no opinion about the statement, "The Chinese will enter the Vietnam war." According to the suggestion, your deliberation about the survey statement should consist of a simple thought experiment: add the antecedent (hypothetically) to your stock of knowledge (or beliefs), and then consider whether or not the consequent is true. Your belief about the conditional should be the same as your hypothetical belief, under this condition, about the consequent.

What happens to the idea of connection on this hypothesis? It is sometimes relevant to the evaluation of a conditional, and sometimes not. If you believe that a casual or logical connection exists, then you will add the consequent to your stock of beliefs along with the antecedent, since the rational man accepts the consequences of his beliefs. On the other hand, if you already believe the consequent (and if you also believe it to be causally independent of the antecedent), then it will remain a part of your stock of beliefs when you add the antecedent, since the rational man does not change his beliefs without reason. In either case, you will affirm the conditional. Thus this answer accounts for the relevance of "connection" when it is relevant without making it a necessary condition of the truth of a conditional.

Ramsey's suggestion covers only the situation in which you have no opinion about the truth value of the antecedent. Can it be generalized? We can of course extend it without problem to the case where you believe or know the antecendent to be true; in this case, no changes need be made in your stock of beliefs. If you already believe that the Chinese will enter the Vietnam conflict, then your belief about the conditional will be just the same as your belief about the statement that the U.S. will use the bomb.

[4] F. P. Ramsey, "General Propositions and Causality" in Ramsey, *Foundations of Mathematics and other Logical Essays* (New York, 1950), pp. 237–257. The suggestion is made on p. 248. Chisholm, *op. cit.*, p. 489, quotes the suggestion and discusses the limitations of the "connection" thesis which it brings out, but he develops it somewhat differently.

What about the case in which you know or believe the antecedent to be false? In this situation, you cannot simply add it to your stock of beliefs without introducing a contradiction. You must make adjustments by deleting or changing those beliefs which conflict with the antecedent. Here, the familiar difficulties begin, of course, because there will be more than one way to make the required adjustments.[5] These difficulties point to the pragmatic problem of counterfactuals, but if we set them aside for a moment, we shall see a rough but general answer to the question we are asking. This is how to evaluate a conditional:

> First, add the antecedent (hypothetically) to your stock of beliefs; second, make whatever adjustments are required to maintain consistency (without modifying the hypothetical belief in the antecedent); finally, consider whether or not the consequent is then true.

It is not particularly important that our answer is approximate—that it skirts the problem of adjustments—since we are using it only as a way of finding truth conditions. It is crucial, however, that the answer not be restricted to some particular context of belief if it is to be helpful in finding a definition of the conditional function. If the conditional is to be understood as a function of the propositions expressed by its component clauses, then its truth value should not in general be dependent on the attitudes which anyone has toward those propositions.

Now that we have found an answer to the question, "How do we decide whether or not we believe a conditional statement?" the problem is to make the transition from belief conditions to truth conditions; that is, to find a set of truth conditions for statements having conditional form which explains why we use the method we do use to evaluate them. The concept of a *possible world* is just what we need to make this transition, since a possible world is the ontological analogue of a stock of hypothetical beliefs. The following set of truth conditions, using this notion, is a first approximation to the account that I shall propose:

> Consider a possible world in which *A* is true, and which otherwise differs minimally from the actual world. "*If A, then B*" *is true* (*false*) *just in case B is true* (*false*) *in that possible world.*

[5] Rescher, *op. cit.*, pp. 11–16, contains a very clear statement and discussion of this problem, which he calls the problem of the ambiguity of belief-contravening hypotheses. He argues that the resolution of this ambiguity depends on pragmatic considerations. Cf. also Goodman's problem of relevant conditions in N. Goodman, *Fact, Fiction, and Forecast* (Cambridge, Mass., 1955), pp. 17–24.

An analysis in terms of possible worlds also has the advantage of providing a ready made apparatus on which to build a formal semantical theory. In making this account of the conditional precise, we use the semantical systems for modal logics developed by Saul Kripke.[6] Following Kripke, we first define a *model structure*. Let M be an ordered triple (K,R,λ). K is to be understood intuitively as the set of all possible worlds; R is the relation of relative possibility which defines the structure. If α and β are possible worlds (members of K), then $\alpha R\beta$ reads "β is possible with respect to α." This means that, where α is the actual world, β is a possible world. R is a reflexive relation; that is, every world is possible with respect to itself. If your modal intuitions so incline you, you may add that R must be transitive, or transitive and symmetrical.[7] The only element that is not a part of the standard modal semantics is λ, a member of K which is to be understood as the *absurd world*—the world in which contradictions and all their consequences are true. It is an isolated element under R; that is, no other world is possible with respect to it, and it is not possible with respect to any other world. The purpose of λ is to allow for an interpretation of "If A, then B" in the case where A is impossible; for this situation one needs an impossible world.

In addition to a model structure, our semantical apparatus includes a *selection function, f*, which takes a proposition and a possible world as arguments and a possible world as its value. The *s*-function selects, for each antecedent A, a particular possible world in which A is true. The *assertion* which the conditional makes, then, is that the consequent is true in the world selected. A conditional is true in the actual world when its consequent is true in the selected world.

Now we can state the semantical rule for the conditional more formally (using the corner, $>$, as the conditional connective):

$A>B$ is true in α if B is true in $f(A,\alpha)$;
$A>B$ is false in α if B is false in $f(A,\alpha)$.

The interpretation shows conditional logic to be an extension of modal logic. Modal logic provides a way of talking about what is true in the actual world, in all possible worlds, or in at least one, unspecified world. The addition of the selection function to the semantics and

[6] S. Kripke, "Semantical Analysis of Modal Logics, I," *Zeitschrift für mathematische Logik und Grundlagen der Mathematik*, vol. 9 (1963), pp. 67–96.
[7] The different restrictions on the relation R provide interpretations for the different modal systems. The system we build on is von Wright's M. If we add the transitivity requirement, then the underlying modal logic of our system is Lewis's S4, and if we add both the transitivity and symmetry requirements, then the modal logic is S5. Cf. S. Kripke, *op. cit.*

the conditional connective to the object language of modal logic provides a way of talking also about what is true in *particular* non-actual possible situations. This is what counterfactuals are: statements about particular counterfactual worlds.

But the world selected cannot be just any world. The *s*-function must meet at least the following conditions. I shall use the following terminology for talking about the arguments and values of *s*-functions: where $f(A,a)=\beta$, A is the *antecedent*, a is the *base world*, and β is the *selected world*.

(1) For all antecedents A and base worlds a, A must be true in $f(A,a)$.

(2) For all antecedents A and base worlds a, $f(A,a)=\lambda$ only if there is no world possible with respect to a in which A is true.

The first condition requires that the antecedent be true in the selected world. This ensures that all statements like "if snow is white, then snow is white" are true. The second condition requires that the absurd world be selected only when the antecedent is impossible. Since everything is true in the absurd world, including contradictions, if the selection function were to choose it for the antecedent A, then "If A, then B and not B" would be true. But one cannot legitimately reach an impossible conclusion from a consistent assumption.

The informal truth conditions that were suggested above required that the world selected *differ minimally* from the actual world. This implies, first, that there are no differences between the actual world and the selected world except those that are required, implicitly or explicitly, by the antecedent. Further, it means that among the alternative ways of making the required changes, one must choose one that does the least violence to the correct description and explanation of the actual world. These are vague conditions which are largely dependent on pragmatic considerations for their application. They suggest, however, that the selection is based on an ordering of possible worlds with respect to their resemblance to the base world. If this is correct, then there are two further formal constraints which must be imposed on the *s*-function.

(3) For all base worlds a and all antecedents A, if A is true in a, then $f(A,a)=a$.

(4) For all base worlds a and all antecedents B and B', if B is true in $f(B',a)$ and B' is true in $f(B,a)$, then $f(B,a)=f(B',a)$.

The third condition requires that the base world be selected if it is among the worlds in which the antecedent is true. Whatever the criteria for evaluating resemblance among possible worlds, there is obviously no other possible world as much like the base world as the base world itself. The fourth condition ensures that the ordering among possible worlds is consistent in the following sense: if any selection established β as prior to β' in the ordering (with respect to a particular base world α), then no other selection (relative to that α) may establish β' as prior to β.[8] Conditions (3) and (4) together ensure that the s-function establishes a total ordering of all selected worlds with respect to each possible world, with the base world preceding all others in the order.

These conditions on the selection function are necessary in order that this account be recognizable as an explication of the conditional, but they are of course far from sufficient to determine the function uniquely. There may be further formal constraints that can plausibly be imposed on the selection principle, but we should not expect to find semantic conditions sufficient to guarantee that there will be a unique s-function for each valuation of non-conditional formulas on a model structure. The questions, "On what basis do we select a selection function from among the acceptable ones?" and "What are the criteria for ordering possible worlds?" are reformulations of the pragmatic problem of counterfactuals, which is a problem in the application of conditional logic. The conditions that I have mentioned above are sufficient, however, to define the semantical notions of validity and consequence for conditional logic.

III. The Formal System

The class of valid formulas of conditional logic according to the definitions sketched in the preceding section, is coextensive with the class of theorems of a formal system, C2. The primitive connectives of C2 are the usual $\supset$ and $\sim$ (with v, &, and $\equiv$ defined as usual), as well as a conditional connective, $>$ (called the corner). Other modal and conditional concepts can be defined in terms of the corner as follows:

$$\Box A =_{DF} \sim A > A$$
$$\Diamond A =_{DF} \sim (A > \sim A)$$
$$A \gtrless B =_{DF} (A>)B \ \& \ (B>A)$$

The rules of inference of C2 are *modus ponens* (if A and $A \supset B$ are theorems, then B is a theorem) and the Gödel rule of necessitation (If A is a theorem, then $\Box A$ is a theorem). There are seven axiom schemata:

---

[8] If $f(A, \alpha) = \beta$, then β is established as prior to all worlds possible with respect to α in which A is true.

(a1) Any tautologous wff (well-formed formula) is an axiom.

(a2) $\Box(A \supset B) \supset (\Box A \supset \Box B)$

(a3) $\Box(A \supset B) \supset (A > B)$

(a4) $\Diamond A \supset .(A > B) \supset \sim(A > \sim B)$

(a5) $A > (B \vee C) \supset .(A > B) \vee (A > C)$

(a6) $(A > B) \supset (A \supset B)$

(a7) $A \gtrless B \supset . \; (A > C) \supset (B > C)$

The conditional connective, as characterized by this formal system, is intermediate between strict implication and the material conditional, in the sense that $\Box(A \supset B)$ entails $A > B$ by (a3) and $A > B$ entails $A \supset B$ by (a6). It cannot, however, be analyzed as a modal operation performed on a material conditional (like Burks' causal implication, for example).[9] The corner lacks certain properties shared by the two traditional implication concepts, and in fact these differences help to explain some peculiarities of counterfactuals. I shall point out three unusual features of the conditional connective.

(1) Unlike both material and strict implication, the conditional corner is a non-transitive connective. That is, from $A > B$ and $B > C$, one cannot infer $A > C$. While this may at first seem surprising, consider the following example: *Premisses.* "If J. Edgar Hoover were today a communist, then he would be a traitor." "If J. Edgar Hoover had been born a Russian, then he would today be a communist." *Conclusion.* "If J. Edgar Hoover had been born a Russian, he would be a traitor." It seems reasonable to affirm these premisses and deny the conclusion.

If this example is not sufficiently compelling, note that the following rule follows from the transitivity rule: From $A > B$ to infer $(A \& C) > B$. But it is obvious that the former rule is invalid; we cannot always strengthen the antecedent of a true conditional and have it remain true. Consider "If this match were struck, it would light," and "If this match had been soaked in water overnight *and* it were struck, it would light."[10]

(2) According to the formal system, the denial of a conditional is equivalent to a conditional with the same antecedent and opposite

[9] A. W. Burks, "The Logic of Causal Propositions," *Mind*, vol. 60 (1951), pp. 363–382. The causal implication connective characterized in this article has the same structure as strict implication. For an interesting philosophical defense of this modal interpretation of conditionals, see B. Mayo, "Conditional Statements," *The Philosophical Review*, vol. 66 (1957), pp. 291–303.

[10] Although the transitivity inference fails, a related inference is of course valid. From $A > B$, $B > C$, and A, one can infer C. Also, note that the biconditional connective is transitive. From $A \gtrless B$ and $B \gtrless C$, one can infer $A \gtrless C$. Thus the biconditional is an equivalence relation, since it is also symmetrical and reflexive.

consequent (provided that the antecedent is not impossible). That is, $\Diamond A - \sim(A > B) \equiv (A > \sim B)$. This explains the fact, noted by both Goodman and Chisholm in their early papers on counterfactuals, that the normal way to contradict a counterfactual is to contradict the consequent, keeping the same antecedent. To deny "If Kennedy were alive today, we wouldn't be in this Vietnam mess," we say, "If Kennedy were alive today, we would so be in this Vietnam mess."

(3) The inference of contraposition, valid for both the truth-functional horseshoe and the strict implication hook, is invalid for the conditional corner. $A > B$ may be true while $\sim B > \sim A$ is false. For an example in support of this conclusion, we take another item from the political opinion survey: "If the U.S. halts the bombing, then North Vietnam will not agree to negotiate." A person would believe that this statement is true if he thought that the North Vietnamese were determined to press for a complete withdrawal of U.S. troops. But he would surely deny the contrapositive, "If North Vietnam agrees to negotiate, then the U.S. will not have halted the bombing." He would believe that a halt in the bombing, and much more, is required to bring the North Vietnamese to the negotiating table.[11]

Examples of these anomalies have been noted by philosophers in the past. For instance, Goodman pointed out that two counterfactuals with the same antecedent and contradictory consequents are "normally meant" as direct negations of each other. He also remarked that we may sometimes assert a conditional and yet reject its contrapositive. He accounted for these facts by arguing that semifactuals—conditionals with false antecedents and true consequents—are for the most part not to be taken literally. "In practice," he wrote, "full counterfactuals affirm, while semifactuals deny, that a certain connection obtains between antecedent and consequent. . . . The practical import of a semifactual is thus different from its literal import."[12] Chisholm also suggested paraphrasing semifactuals before analyzing them. "Even if you were to sleep all morning, you would be tired" is to be read "It is false that if you were to sleep all morning, you would not be tired."[13]

A separate and nonconditional analysis for semi-factuals is necessary to save the "connection" theory of counterfactuals in the face of the anomolies we have discussed, but it is a baldly *ad hoc*

---

[11] Although contraposition fails, *modus tolens* is valid for the conditional: from $A > B$ and $\sim B$, one can infer $\sim A$.

[12] Goodman, *op. cit.*, pp. 15, 32.

[13] Chisholm, *op. cit.*, p. 492.

maneuver. Any analysis can be saved by paraphrasing the counter-examples. The theory presented in Sect. II avoids this difficulty by denying that the conditional can be said, in general, to assert a connection of any particular kind between antecedent and consequent. It is, of course, the structure of inductive relations and casual connections which make counterfactuals and semifactuals true or false, but they do this by determining the relationships among possible worlds, which in turn determine the truth values of conditionals. By treating the relation between connection and conditionals as an indirect relation in this way, the theory is able to give a unified account of conditionals which explains the variations in their behavior in different contexts.

IV. THE LOGICAL PROBLEM: GENERAL CONSIDERATIONS

The traditional strategy for attacking a problem like the logical problem of conditionals was to find an *analysis*, to show that the unclear or objectionable phrase was dispensable, or replaceable by something clear and harmless. Analysis was viewed by some as an *unpacking*—a making manifest of what was latent in the concept; by others it was seen as the *replacement* of a vague idea by a precise one, adequate to the same purposes as the old expression, but free of its problems. The semantic theory of conditionals can also be viewed either as the construction of a concept to replace an unclear notion of ordinary language, or as an *explanation* of a commonly used concept. I see the theory in the latter way: no recommendation or stipulation is intended. This does not imply, however, that the theory is meant as a description of linguistic usage. What is being explained is not the rules governing the use of an English word, but the structure of a concept. Linguistic facts—what we would say in this or that context, and what sounds odd to the native speaker—are relevant as evidence, since one may presume that concepts are to some extent mirrored in language.

The "facts," taken singly, need not be decisive. A recalcitrant counterexample may be judged a deviant use or a different sense of the word. We can claim that a paraphrase is necessary, or even that ordinary language is systematically mistaken about the concept we are explaining. There are, of course, different senses and times when "ordinary language" goes astray, but such *ad hoc* hypotheses and qualifications diminish both the plausibility and the explanatory force of a theory. While we are not irrevocably bound to the linguistic facts, there are no "don't cares"—contexts of use with which we are not concerned, since any context can be relevant as evidence for or against an analysis. A general interpretation which avoids dividing senses and accounts for the behavior of a concept in many contexts fits the familiar pattern of scientific explanation in which diverse, seemingly unlike surface phenomena are seen as deriving from some common source. For these reasons, I take it as a strong point in favor of the semantic theory that it treats the conditional as a univocal concept.

V. PRAGMATIC AMBIGUITY

I have argued that the conditional connective is semantically unambiguous. It is obvious, however, that the context of utterance, the purpose of the assertion, and the beliefs of the speaker or his community may make a difference to the interpretation of a counter-factual. How do we reconcile the ambiguity of conditional sentences with the univocity of the conditional concept? Let us look more closely at the notion of ambiguity.

A sentence is ambiguous if there is more than one proposition which it may properly be interpreted to express. Ambiguity may be syntactic (if the sentence has more than one grammatical structure), semantic (if one of the words has more than one meaning), or pragmatic (if the interpretation depends directly on the context of use). The first two kinds of ambiguity are perhaps more familiar, but the third kind is probably the most common in natural languages. Any sentence involving pronouns, tensed verbs, articles or quantifiers is prag-matically ambiguous. For example, the proposition expressed by "L'état, c'est moi" depends on who says it; "Do it now" may be good or bad advice depending on when it is said; "Cherchez la femme" is ambiguous since it contains a definite description, and the truth conditions for "All's well that ends well" depends on the domain of discourse. If the theory presented above is correct, then we may add conditional sentences to this list. The truth conditions for "If wishes were horses, then beggers would ride" depend on the specification of an s-function.[14]

The grounds for treating the ambiguity of conditional sentences as pragmatic rather than semantic are the same as the grounds for treating the ambiguity of quantified sentences as pragmatic: simplicity and systematic coherence. The truth conditions for quantified state-ments vary with a change in the domain of discourse, but there is

---

[14] I do not wish to pretend that the notions needed to define ambiguity and to make the distinction between pragmatic and semantic ambiguity (e.g., "proposi-tion," and "meaning") are precise. They can be made precise only in the context of semantic and pragmatic theories. But even if it is unclear, in general, what pragmatic ambiguity is, it is clear, I hope, that my examples are cases of it.

a single structure to these truth conditions which remains constant for every domain. The semantics for classical predicate logic brings out this common structure by giving the universal quantifier a single meaning and making the domain a parameter of the interpretation. In a similar fashion, the semantics for conditional logic brings out the common structure of the truth conditions for conditional statements by giving the connective a single meaning and making the selection function a parameter of the interpretation.

Just as we can communicate effectively using quantified sentences without explicitly specifying a domain, so we can communicate effectively using conditional sentences without explicitly specifying an s-function. This suggests that there are further rules beyond those set down in the semantics, governing the use of conditional sentences. Such rules are the subject matter of a *pragmatics* of conditionals. Very little can be said, at this point, about pragmatic rules for the use of conditionals since the logic has not advanced beyond the propositional stage, but I shall make a few speculative remarks about the kinds of research which may provide a framework for treatment of this problem, and related pragmatic problems in the philosophy of science.

(1) If we had a functional logic with a conditional connective, it is likely that $(\forall x)(Fx > Gx)$ would be a plausible candidate for the form of a law of nature. A law of nature says, not just that every actual F is a G, but further that for every possible F, if it were an F, it would be a G. If this is correct, then Hempel's confirmation paradox does not arise, since "All ravens are black" is not logically equivalent to "All non-black things are non-ravens." Also, the relation between counterfactuals and laws becomes clear: laws support counterfactuals because they entail them. "If this dove were a raven, it would be black" is simply an instantiation of "All ravens are black."[15]

(2) Goodman has argued that the pragmatic problem of counterfactuals is one of a cluster of closely related problems concerning induction and confirmation. He locates the source of these difficulties in the general problem of projectability, which can be stated roughly as follows: when can a predicate be validly projected from one set of cases to others? or when is a hypothesis confirmed by its positive instances? Some way of distinguishing between natural predicates

---

[15] For a discussion of the relation of laws to counterfactuals, see E. Nagel, *Structure of Science* (New York, 1961), pp. 47–78. For a recent discussion of the paradoxes of confirmation by the man who discovered them, see C. G. Hempel, "Recent Problems of Induction" in *Mind and Cosmos*, ed. by R. G. Colodny (Pittsburgh, 1966), pp. 112–134.

and those which are artificially constructed is needed. If a theory of projection such as Goodman envisions were developed, it might find a natural place in a pragmatics of conditionals. Pragmatic criteria for measuring the inductive properties of predicates might provide pragmatic criteria for ordering possible worlds.[16]

(3) There are some striking structural parallels between conditional logic and conditional probability functions, which suggests the possibility of a connection between inductive logic and conditional logic. A probability assignment and an s-function are two quite different ways to describe the inductive relations among propositions; a theory which draws a connection between them might be illuminating for both.[17]

VI. CONCLUSION: EMPIRICISM AND POSSIBLE WORLDS

Writers of fiction and fantasy sometimes suggest that imaginary worlds have a life of their own beyond the control of their creators. Pirandello's six characters, for example, rebelled against their author and took the story out of his hands. The skeptic may be inclined to suspect that this suggestion is itself fantasy. He believes that nothing goes into a fictional world, or a possible world, unless it is put there by decision or convention; it is a creature of invention and not discovery. Even the fabulist Tolkien admits that Faërie is a land "full of wonder, but not of information."[18]

For similar reasons, the empiricist may be uncomfortable about a theory which treats counterfactuals as literal statements about non-actual situations. Counterfactuals are often contingent, and contingent statements must be supported by evidence. But evidence can be gathered, by us at least, only in this universe. To satisfy the empiricist, I must show how possible worlds, even if the product of convention, can be subjects of empirical investigation.

There is no mystery to the fact that I can partially define a possible world in such a way that I am ignorant of some of the determinate truths in that world. One way I can do this is to attribute to it features

---

[16] Goodman, op. cit., especially Ch. IV.

[17] Several philosophers have discussed the relation of conditional propositions to conditional probabilities. See R. C. Jeffrey, "If," The Journal of Philosophy, vol. 61 (1964), pp. 702–703, and E. W. Adams, "Probability and the Logic of Conditionals" in Aspects of Inductive Logic, ed. by J. Hintikka and P. Suppes (Amsterdam, 1966), pp. 265–316. I hope to present elsewhere my method of drawing the connection between the two notions, which differs from both of these.

[18] J. R. Tolkien, "On Fairy Stories" in The Tolkien Reader (New York, 1966), p. 3.

of the actual world which are unknown to me. Thus I can say, "I am thinking of a possible world in which the population of China is just the same, on each day, as it is in the actual world." *I* am making up this world—it is a pure product of my intentions—but there are already things true in it which I shall never know.

Conditionals do implicitly, and by convention, what is done explicitly by stipulation in this example. It is because counterfactuals are generally about possible worlds which are very much like the actual one, and defined in terms of it, that evidence is so often relevant to their truth. When I wonder, for example, what would have happened if I had asked my boss for a raise yesterday, I am wondering about a possible world that I have already roughly picked out. It has the same history, up to yesterday, as the actual world, the same boss with the same dispositions and habits. The main difference is that in that world, yesterday I asked the boss for a raise. Since I do not know everything about the boss's habits and dispositions in the actual world, there is a lot that I do not know about how he acts in the possible world that I have chosen, although I might find out by watching him respond to a similar request from another, or by asking his secretary about his mood yesterday. These bits of information about the actual world would not be decisive, of course, but they would be relevant, since they tell me more about the non-actual situation that I have selected.

If I make a conditional statement—subjunctive or otherwise—and the antecedent turns out to be true, then whether I know it or not, I have said something about the actual world, namely that the consequent is true in it. If the antecedent is false, then I have said something about a particular counterfactual world, even if I believe the antecedent to be true. The conditional provides a set of conventions for selecting possible situations which have a specified relation to what actually happens. This makes it possible for statements about unrealized possibilities to tell us, not just about the speaker's imagination, but about the world.

Yale University

V

Goodman's Nominalism

ALAN HAUSMAN AND CHARLES ECHELBARGER

IN this paper we shall show that (1) Goodman's ontology, as presented in *The Structure of Appearance*,[1] cannot account for facts for which any adequate ontology must account, and (2) any attempt to account for these facts within his nominalistic ontology must end in failure. With respect to (1) we shall show that *two* things, e.g., two spots, which, presystematically speaking, are unquestionably different, are absolutely identical within the system of *SA*. That is, the fact that the two are different cannot be preserved within that system. Since the difficulty seems to involve Goodman's analysis of identity, it appears that a new analysis of the notion would enable the system to accommodate the fact in question. Our second major argument, (2), is that this accommodation cannot be made within any conceivable extension of Goodman's nominalistic ontology.

I

Goodman's fundamental ontological idea is that there is only *one kind* of entity, namely individuals. His opponent, the platonist, claims that there are at least *two* kinds, namely individuals and classes of them. An individual is "simply a segment of the world of experience, and its boundaries may be complex to any degree."[2] But whatever one chooses as the individuals of his ontological scheme, these entities can be sharply distinguished from classes. Precisely how Goodman conceives of the notion of a class need not concern us here. For whatever reason, he finds it unintelligible. As a philosopher, however, his task is the same as the platonist's. He must give an ontological account of our world and, in so doing, solve at least some of the traditional philosophical puzzles. His method is to build a language which, he hopes, will enable him to do both. This language is the

---

[1] Nelson Goodman, *The Structure of Appearance* (Cambridge, Harvard University Press, 1951; a second edition was published in 1966 by The Bobbs-Merrill Company). This work will be referred to as *SA*. Page references without parenthesis are to the first edition, those in parenthesis to the corresponding pages in the second edition.

[2] *SA*, p. 42 (dropped in the second edition).

calculus of individuals (CI) supplemented by a small stock of primitive predicates.[3] The spirit of Goodman's method is that of Carnap's *Aufbau*; the language, radically different. Carnap is a platonist; Goodman must reconstruct the world with a severely restricted logical apparatus.[4]

CI is a virtual isomorph of the class calculus easily constructed within a platonistic language such as *Principia Mathematica*. Its single primitive predicate is the two-place relation sign 'O,' read "overlaps." Speaking presystematically, two entities overlap if they have some common "content." Logically speaking, the predicate 'O' is the *CI* isomorph of the familiar *Principia* predicate "class product." Ontologically, the notion of content is far from clear. Since it plays a crucial role in Goodman's ontology, and in our discussion, we shall have much more to say about it later.

CI contains only one kind of variable whose values are whatever one may choose as individuals. These values include not only simple (atomic) individuals, but *sums*, which in *CI* are the correlates of *Principia* classes. The sum of two individuals is that individual which "exactly and completely exhausts both."[5] Rather than define a three place sum predicate, Goodman introduces sums by means of a descriptive function:

(1) $x+y =_\text{DF} (\imath z)[(\forall w)((O(w,z)) \equiv (O(w,x) \vee O(w,y)))]$.

In words, the sum of x and y is that individual z such that whatever overlaps z also overlaps either x or y, and conversely. Next he adopts the statement

(2) $(\exists z)(z=x+y)$

as a postulate, thereby guaranteeing that every two individuals have a sum, i.e., the description is always successful. Other predicates coresponding to familiar ones of the class calculus are easily definable. An example is the *CI* correlate of '$\subset$':

(3) $x<y =_\text{DF} (\forall z) [O(z,x) \supset O(z,y)]$.

In words, "x is a *part* of y" means by definition that "any individual which overlaps x also overlaps y." Most important for our purposes, identity of individuals is transcribed as follows:

[3] The language was first described in detail by Goodman and Henry S. Leonard in "The Calculus of Individuals and its Uses," *The Journal of Symbolic Logic*, vol. 5 (1940), pp. 45–55.

[4] For a detailed discussion of many of the points in this section see the forthcoming "Goodman's Ontology" in *Carnap and Goodman: Two Formalists*, by A. Hausman and F. Wilson, to be published as the third volume of the series *Iowa Publications in Philosophy*.

[5] *SA*, pp. 45–46 (50–51). Formulas (1)–(4) which follow are discussed on pp. 44–46 (49–51).

(4) $x=y$ =DF $(\forall z)\, [O(z,x)\equiv O(z,y)]$.

Two individuals are identical if and only if whatever overlaps the one overlaps the other and conversely.

CI is, of course, an empty shell as it stands, an axiomatic system in need of interpretation. Since his primary task is ontological, Goodman must provide an interpretation which will enable him to analyze ordinary objects and the relations among them. He chooses *qualia* as simple individuals. A quale is a phenomenal quality, e.g., the color manifested by a momentary spot in a visual field. Such spots, which are *not* continuants, will be called herein *ordinary things*. Qualia have all the essential earmarks of universals: they are both recognizable and repeatable.[6] What, then, is the spot? Consider two spots of the same shade of color presented simultaneously in the visual field, one to the left of the other. As Goodman analyzes them, each spot consists of a color, a *place*, and a *time* quale. Each spot has the same color and time quale, but they differ in place qualia. Place and time qualia (in the case of two spots of the same color in the same place at different times) thus serve to individuate any two given spots. *Presystematically* all appears well. How will the spots be represented in his systematic language?

CI, remember, is the fundamental logical apparatus of this language. The values of its variables are qualia, i.e., color, place, and time qualities, and their sums. How shall we interpret '*O*'? It is not taken as the name of a relation or a class but, rather, as a syncategorematic term, meaningful in context only.[7] *Thus the only existents represented in the system are qualia and their sums.* An ordinary thing cannot be a simple quale. Thus it must be a sum. Rather obviously, however, not all sums are ordinary things. For not only do any two individuals have a sum, but a sum may (indeed, must) exist whether or not there is an ordinary thing consisting of the sum's simple *parts* (in the sense of (3)). To see this clearly, consider a world consisting of just three spots, whose qualia are c_1, p_1, t_1; and c_1, p_2, t_1; and c_1, p_1, t_2, respectively. The sum $c_1+p_2+t_2$ exists, but is not a spot. Yet, if there were such a spot, the sum expressions in the language would be exactly the same. Therefore, some way must be devised to distinguish those sums

[6] *Ibid.*, pp. 98, 147 ff. (132, 189 ff.).

[7] Considering the importance of this subject, Goodman says very little about it in *SA*. See, however, pp. 30 ff. (33 ff.), especially p. 34 (37) where, in the discussion of nominalism, reference is made to his joint article with Quine, "Steps Toward a Constructive Nominalism," *The Journal of Symbolic Logic*, vol. 12 (1947), pp. 105–122. This article, as well as others cited in *SA* by Quine, make it clear that all predicates of individuals are to be construed syncategorematically. See also pp. 203–204 (251–253) and 211–214 (260–264), especially p. 212 (261).

which are from those which are not ordinary things. Before proceeding to this device, some preliminary comments must be made.

At the heart of Goodman's nominalism as he himself describes it is the principle that entities differ only insofar as their "content" differs.[8] An entity thus *consists* of its "content" and nothing more. Taking the principle in one way, it expresses a cardinal idea of ontology. If two ordinary objects differ, the analysis of one must yield an entity which the analysis of the other does not yield. By itself, however, the principle legislates nothing about what there is. But, once one decides upon the content of the world, one must apply the principle in terms of those existents. Goodman decides that the world's content is qualia and their sums. Since predicates are interpreted syncategorematically, this is its *only* content. Rather obviously, then, it appears that any attempt to distinguish sums which are from sums which are not ordinary things is doomed to failure in at least this respect: those sums which are ordinary things will have the same content that they would have had if they had been mere sums. Let us see.

What, speaking informally, is the difference between a mere sum and an ordinary thing? As Goodman sees it, an ordinary thing consists of qualia which are *together* in a way in which the qualia which are mere parts ($<$) of a sum are not together. Thus he introduces a primitive predicate 'W,' read "with," such that "$W(x,y)$" is true if x and y are together. It is now easy to define a predicate, given the proper axioms for 'W,' which applies to a sum when its parts are *with* one another:

(5) $Cm(x)$ =DF $(\forall y)(\forall z) [[(y+z<x)\&(y\|z)] \supset W(y,z)]$[9]

In words, x is a *complex* if each of its *discrete* ($\|$), i.e., nonoverlapping, parts are with one another. *Concreta*, i.e., ordinary things, are just those complexes that are with no other individual:

(6) $\cent(x)$ =DF $Cm(x)\&(\forall y)\sim W(x,y)$.[10]

Thus, the expanded definiens of (6) contains W- statements, and it is easily shown that a sum $c+p+t$, where c, p, and t are a color, a place, and a time, respectively, is a concretum if and only if "$W(c,p+t)$" is true.[11] However, since 'W' does not represent any content, its application in no way adds to the content of a sum. It follows that the distinction Goodman draws between sums that are ordinary things and

---

[8] *Ibid.*, pp. 32–33 (36–37). See also the discussion in Goodman's "A World of Individuals" in *The Problem of Universals* (Notre Dame, The University of Notre Dame Press, 1956).

[9] *SA*, p. 180 (227).

[10] *Ibid.*, p. 183 (230).

[11] This follows from the axioms for 'W,' p. 179 (225–226).

sums that are not is merely verbal. There is no corresponding distinction in content. This anomaly can be grasped best by means of an example which will fully document our claim that there are facts for which Goodman cannot account, and for which any adequate ontology must account.

Consider two spots α and β which, as we ordinarily speak and think, are continuing things (this, of course, does not commit one to an ontology with continuants). Goodman's phenomenalistic ontology does not contain continuants. In platonistic ontologies without continuants α and β are taken to be the class of their temporal cross sections. In Goodman's system, sums take the place of classes, and cross sections of things like α and β are concreta, i.e., sums to which the defined predicate 'ϕ' applies.[12] Thus α and β are each a sum of sums. This leads to trouble.

Assume that at t_1 α and β have the same color quale c_1, and α is at p_1 at a distance d to the left of β at p_2. At t_1, then, there exist two ordinary things, in the sense in which we use the term, A and B, which, speaking presystematically, are (in a sense to be analyzed) "parts" of α and β respectively. Goodman would represent A and B by the *sum expressions* "$c_1+p_1+t_1$" and "$c_1+p_2+t_1$."[13] Assume that d is the diameter of a circle with α and β on opposite ends; let α and β move clockwise around the circle one and one-half times at constant speed. α ends at p_2 and β at p_1. Each will have moved through the same places and exists at the same times; the color remains constant. The following difficulty results. α is the sum of the concretum A and a whole series of others, i.e., a sum of sums; β is the sum of B and a whole series of other concreta, thus also a sum of sums. But the sums are *identical* by (4)! That is, the systematic correlate of α is a sum which is identical to the sum which is the systematic correlate of β, for each contains the same qualia. *Yet we know that α and β are two and not one.* α could have existed without β having existed and conversely, just as the sum which represents the analysis of both could have existed without either α or β having existed (as long as each of the qualia in the sum in question is a part ($<$) of some concretum or other). We conclude that there

---

[12] On pp. 94–95 (128–131) Goodman discusses the relation between an object and the totality of its presentations, and claims that it is *part* to *whole* which, in his systematic language, amounts to making cross sections of what we ordinarily consider to be continuing spots, sums which are part ($<$) of larger sums. He claims also that identity of what we ordinarily consider to be a continuing object is *additive*.

[13] See for example, p. 195 (244) where he refers to a place-time (which is a complex) by the sum description. Where there is no danger of ambiguity, we shall also use 'α,' 'β,' 'A,' and 'B' as names for the *systematic correlates* of α, β, A, and B. Otherwise, we shall speak of the correlate of α, etc.

are facts for which any adequate ontology must account, namely, the difference between α and β, for which Goodman cannot account.

A simplification of the example will help. Let A and B remain as before, and consider two other momentary color spots at t_2, C and D, C with color c_1 at place p_1, D with color c_1 at place p_2. Let α (upon analysis) be the sum of the two momentary spots A and D (whose systematic analysis makes them each sums), and β, the sum of B and C.[14] Systematically, then, α is represented by "$(c_1+p_1+t_1)+(c_1+p_2+t_2)$," and β by "$(c_1+p_2+t_1)+(c_1+p_1+t_2)$." The sums are identical. Thus two things, α and β, which are unquestionably different, are systematically analyzed as one entity, and represented in the language of the system by one expression.

In reply, Goodman might remind us that a predicate 'W' applies to the parts of the sums which "are" A, B, C, and D, respectively, and that these different applications show that α and β are not the same spot. That is, α and β are "made up of" different concreta. Pre-systematically all is well. But how do these facts show themselves in the language? Certainly the four statements "$W(c_1,p_1+t_1)$," "$W(c_1,p_2+t_2)$," "$W(c_1,p_2+t_1)$" and "$W(c_1,p_1+t_2)$" are true. However, two difficulties immediately present themselves. (i) In some ontologies where predicate signs refer to properties and relations, true sentences such as "$W(c_1,p_1+t_1)$" are taken to be about (or, even, to refer to) states of affairs (facts). The content of such states of affairs includes the properties and relations, e.g., W. But in Goodman's ontology the only existents are simple qualia and their sums, and both are *individuals*. That is both are, or, in Goodman's case, *could be* represented by *undefined* constants or names of the lowest logical type (the fact that Goodman uses "defined" constants, i.e., descriptions, to refer to sums is, in this sense, merely a convenience). Thus the systematic correlates of A, B, C, and D are all individuals; so, then, are the correlates of α and β. (ii) The fact that the four sentences are true has no significance for the determination of whether the correlates of α and β are identical, insofar as identity is transcribed by (4). (4) makes no reference to any predicative contexts other than 'O.' Thus the fact that α and β are "made up of" different concreta plays no role in determining whether they are identical. The expression which represents α, as we just saw, is not "$W(c_1,p_1+t_1)\&W(c_1,p_2+t_2)$," but rather, "$(c_1+p_1+t_1)+(c_1+p_2+t_2)$." Since the same expression represents β, the difficulty remains.

---

[14] In terms of our previous example, this makes α and β the sums of the concreta which constitute the beginning and end points of their motion around the circle (with the obvious correction for time elapsed).

There is a second possible reply, also inadequate. Suppose that at t_1 A, which is a part of the systematic correlate of α, stands in a relation R to some concretum ψ, while at that same time B, which is a part of the systematic correlate of β, does not stand in R to ψ but in S to yet another concretum, γ; assume finally that A does not stand in S to γ. The idea is this: the systematic correlates of α and β will now be distinguished by the fact that a part of the correlate of α, namely, A, stands in relation to something to which a part of the correlate of β, namely, B, does not stand, and conversely. There are two objections to this device: (i) it now seems that we must include as part of the content of the correlates of α and β at least the concreta to which their parts stand in relations, as well as A, B, etc.[15] Call these new correlates α' and β'. Are α' and β' nonidentical by (4)? They are not. α' and β' still contain as parts all the concreta (sums) which the *original* correlates contained, plus new concreta; for example, A is still a part of *both* α' and β'. Thus any concretum to which A stands in a relation, if made part of the content of α', must also be made part of the content of β'. The original correlates of α and β are identical, every part of one is a part of the other; hence, any relation in which a part of one stands a part of the other also stands. It follows that α' and β' are also identical.[16] (ii) One may object to our objection by claiming that, after all, A is a concretum and stands in R to ψ, but there really is no concretum in the correlate of β that stands in that relation. But this claim is false. The correlate of β, surprisingly, *does* contain the concretum A (we shall return to this point presently). And if the claim is that the original correlates of α and β *do* contain different content, i.e., different concreta, then there is no need to bring in the relations in which these concreta stand. As we have already seen, however, the fact that A is a concretum does not help resolve the difficulty.

If any doubt exists about the nature of the above examples, it should be pointed out that Goodman himself considers a case which exactly parallels them in all relevant respects. The context of his discussion, which is not our main interest here, is what he calls *uniform qualification*. Briefly, the idea of *uniform qualification* is this: (1) A quale a is said to K-qualify a complex if it is a part ($<$) of that complex. (2) Goodman then considers entities called *compounds*

---

[15] Goodman could not, of course, count the relation itself as part of the content of the correlates without violating the central tenets of nominalism.

[16] Our objection to this view is in spirit the same as one made long ago by Russell. See "On the Relation of Universals and Particulars" in *Logic and Knowledge: Essays* 1901–1950, ed. R. C. Marsh (London, 1956). Relations cannot individuate two things, for if they are identical they stand in the same relations and if they are not, they must be two in order for them to stand in different relations.

which are "larger than" complexes, e.g., sums of concreta. Such a compound is, for example, "an extended visual presentation b" which "has some one color c throughout."[17] c is said to uniformly qualify b. The problem he sets for himself is the definition of the predicate "uniformly qualifies" ("Ku"). One proposal is that

> . . . [the quale] x is required to K-qualify not every part of y [a compound] but only every major complex of y, where a major complex or *section* of an individual is any complex contained in that individual, but not in any other complex contained in that individual.[18]

Then he says

> Suppose that p_1+t_1 and p_2+t_2 and p_1+t_2 and p_2+t_1 are place-times, and that color c_1 occurs at p_1+t_1 and at p_2+t_2 but not at the other two place-times. Let y be the sum of the color-spot-moments $c_1+p_1+t_1$ and $c_1+p_2+t_2$. Clearly c_1 uniformly qualifies y; but does the predicate "uniformly qualifies", if defined as suggested in the preceding paragraph, apply between c_1 and y? Certainly y contains no other tricomplexes, for no other sum of three of the five qualia contained in y is a complex. But, strangely, y has other sections. Place-times p_1+t_2 and p_2+t_1 are complexes, and are parts of y since they are made up of qualia contained in y; and neither is part of another complex contained in y. Hence each is a section of y. Yet of course neither of them is K-qualified by c_1. Thus, although c_1 uniformly qualifies y, it does not K-qualify all sections of y; and so our proposed definition is shown to be unsatisfactory.[19]

We, too, find the example strange. Goodman does not explain why he thinks it so, but we shall. Indeed, it is strange in a far more interesting sense than Goodman may have suspected.

Consider his example. His concern is that the sum of two concreta, i.e., the sum of a color-spot-moment which exists at t_1 and a spot of the same color which exists at a different place at t_2, "contains" other complexes. Recall our simplified example of α and β. As we defined it, α is precisely the compound which he discusses. To make our same point in his own terms, we need only consider a third concretum, C of our simplified example, which is the sum $c_1+p_1+t_2$. Goodman tells us that α literally "contains" the concretum C. Indeed, it is, to use his terms, a *section* of y (our α). Consider the implications. A spot A, presented at t_1, together with another of the same color, presented at t_2, literally "contains" a third spot! This is not merely strange; we find it absurd.[20] In a sense, we don't even understand what it means.

[18] *Ibid.*, p. 192 (239–240). The phrase "but not . . . individual," was added in the second edition.
[19] *Ibid.*, p. 192 (240). The fourth sentence of the quoted passage reads ". . . six qualia . . ." in the first edition, but was corrected in the second.
[20] A further aspect of the strangeness is that whether or not the concretum C exists, the content of the world is still the same if α exists.

But we do understand, and shall explain in Sect. II, why the ontology of his system permits such absurdities.[21]

The most obvious step toward removing the difficulty, at least with respect to the representation (systematic language), seems to be to redefine '=' to include 'W' contexts. In platonistic languages such as *Principia* '=' is usually defined in a way which makes reference to all predicative contexts. Thus

(7) $x=y$ =DF $(\forall f)[f(x) \equiv f(y)]$,

the Russell-Leibniz analysis of identity, says that two individuals are identical if they have *all* their properties, relational and nonrelational, in common. Goodman's definition seems unduly restrictive, especially in the light of the difficulties we have uncovered. Let us see, then, whether a new analysis of identity will help resolve them.

II

In one way, it is quite clear why Goodman states his analysis of identity solely in terms of 'O'-contexts. He holds that simple qualia and their sums are the only existents, and both are individuals. If this were the case, then since 'O' is the only primitive predicate of *CI*, (4) would be a perfectly adequate definition of '=.' Our claim is that there are some entities such that (4) does not completely determine their identity of nonidentity; these entities cannot be either qualia or their sums, and a new analysis of identity is called for. Thus we believe that no emendation to (4) can resolve the difficulties we have raised. This we shall now show.

First, consider the previously proposed inclusion of 'W'-contexts:

(8) $x=y$ =DF$(\forall z)$ $[O(z, x) \equiv O(z,y)]\&(\forall u)[W(u,x) \equiv W(u,y)]$.

Recall that in the definition of "$\cent$," (6), Goodman stipulates that x is a concretum if and only if x is a complex and with no individual. That Goodman must bar concreta from W-ties is evident from the fact that, were he not to do so, there would be no systematic device for distinguishing complexes from concreta. A complex, as defined by (5), may be such that all its parts ($<$) are with one another, and yet be nonconcrete, i.e., not an ordinary thing; even simple qualia are complexes. One result of (6), however, is that the proposed amendment becomes superfluous since, where x and y are concreta, "$(\forall u)[W(u,x) \equiv W(u,y)]$" is vacuously true.

---

[21] It is ironic that an ontology which, in one sense, is an extreme example of atomism, is *holistic*, since the sum of two momentary spots literally contains a third spot. But perhaps it is obvious that an ontology which either contains no real relations or whose primary relations are internal (O is surely internal in the relevant sense) is bound to be holistic.

In the example we described in Sect. I, α and β are not complexes, since not all of their parts are tied by W. From this and Goodman's theorem

(9) $W(x,y) \supset [Cm(x) \& Cm(y)]$, [22]

it follows that α and β, as represented in his language, are also identical even with the proposed amendment, since nothing is with either.

Another plausible amendment is as follows: Since α and β are non-complex entities whose constituents are concreta, it seems that one could show their nonidentity be exhibiting the fact that α contains concreta which β does not contain. Then, beside the O-requirement, entities like α and β are identical if every concrete part of the one is a concrete part of the other and conversely. Obviously this will not do. Concreta are mere sums, and the correlates of α and β are identical sums. Or, to say the same thing differently, since the sum of two concreta may literally contain a third concretum as a part (as we pointed out in Sect. 1), the proposal must fail: for the correlate of a contains every concretum that the correlate of B contains, and conversely.

By now it should be obvious that no addition of a clause containing a reference to W will enable Goodman to escape the difficulty, since a necessary and sufficient condition for identity of *qualia* and *sums* is indeed provided by the definiens of (4). At the risk of belaboring the obvious, let us contrast Goodman's language with the platonistic *Principia*, in which identity is transcribed by (7). (7) transcribes the idea that identical individuals have *all* their properties in common and stand in all the same relations. Suppose, however, that there is some special property or relation, e.g., as some have argued for spatial relations, such that if an individual x has it, another individual y cannot, and conversely. One might then introduce '$=$' analyzed in terms of that property or relation alone. Of course, one might argue, correctly we think, that this analysis of '$=$' would not transcribe our presystematic notion of identity. '$=$' would, on the proposed definition, simply mean "identity in a respect" which, if x and y were so identical, would be sufficient *as a matter of fact* to guarantee identity in all other respects.

Although it may appear that Goodman is in an analagous position, he in fact is not. If the analogy were complete, O would be the special relation in question, (4) would be the special definition of "identity in a respect," and 'W' would stand as the other relation which two individuals x and y would have to the same individuals if x and y were identical in the respect in question. However, the success of the

[22] *SA*, p. 181 (227).

analogy depends upon the fact that O applies to the same kind of individuals as does W. Otherwise, of course, from the fact that two individuals overlap the same individuals nothing follows about their W-relations. If the individual variables of a system range over numbers and oranges, one may find numerical predicates which guarantee the identity of numbers. But since other predicates of the system will be true of oranges and not numbers, the application of numerical predicates will have no bearing on the question of whether "two" oranges are identical, and conversely. We suggest that qualia and their sums on the one hand, and ordinary things on the other, are radically different kinds of individuals. If they were of the same kind, the problem over α and β would not arise. But 'ϕ' no more applies to sums than "Valencia" does to numbers. Small wonder, then, that the difficulty arises and cannot be resolved as the system stands.

It would seem, then, that in order to escape the difficulty we have noted, Goodman will be faced with one of two alternatives equally repugnant to his nominalism. (i) 'W' may be treated as the name of an entity which forms part of the content of an ordinary thing. This, of course, would grant ontological status to a nonindividual. (ii) If he wishes to continue to treat 'W' as a syncategorematic term, he must introduce a new *kind* of "complex" individual as the systematic correlate of ordinary things. Though this is formally possible[23] it is tantamount to giving up the view that there is only one kind of thing, since the notion of individual is stretched to the breaking point.

III

Our principle objection to Goodman's nominalistic system is that it cannot account for facts which must be accounted for by an adequate ontology.[24] One reason for this is that he refuses to let the predicates of his system refer to nonindividuals. One might object, however, that our objection misses the whole point of treating predicates as syncategorematic terms. But, if we may put it this way, just how do such terms "mean"? We can think of two likely answers. (i) One might claim that what distinguishes α from β in our example is the *application*

[23] For a more complete discussion, see Hausman's "Goodman's Ontology,"*op. cit.*
[24] It has been suggested to us that Goodman might not feel himself under any obligation to distinguish systematically two continuing things which are presystematically distinct. The text does not bear out this contention. For one thing, he explicitly states in *SA* (pp. 93–95; pp. 127–130 of the new edition) that a goal of the book is to provide a systematic analysis of what we ordinarily take to be continuing physical objects. For another, he states that systematic translations of presystematically true sentences *which we care about* must preserve truth value (pp. 11 and 20; pp. 12 and 22 of the new edition). We have provided a true sentence about the continuants which are cared about, namely "α is not identical with β" which is false when systematically translated.

of the predicate '$\not\!\!c$' to different sums in α and β. We have already pointed out that this is not so, since every quale in α is in β, and conversely. But even if, *per impossible*, this worked, the difference in content between the two would be mind-dependent. It is human beings who apply predicates; and the consequence is that α and β are different in virtue of the fact that they are called different by a perceiver.[25] To avoid this consequence, one must provide a *ground* for the difference by letting predicates refer to nonindividuals. The claim that one cannot fully analyze ordinary things without bringing in minds is, of course, the classical position of idealism.

(ii) One may claim that although predicates do not denote, they connote; thus 'O' connotes all pairs of individuals that overlap, and 'W' all pairs that are together. The difference between a mere sum and a concretum, then, is that the predicates applying to them have different extensions. This does not work. The predicate "*sum*" applies to all qualia, since every quale is the sum of itself with itself, and "*Cm*" has all qualia in its extension, since every quale is with some other quale.[26] It is true that the classes of ordered pairs which constitute the extension differ, but Goodman disavows classes; hence, it is difficult to see how he could give the predicates such an interpretation. For him, the extension of predicates if we understand correctly, is reckoned in terms of individuals. Again, one may object that "*sum*" has in its extension individuals other than simple qualia, e.g., the sum of all qualia in the universe, which "*Cm*" does not have in its extension. But if Goodman refuses to say that the two extensions reduce to the same entities, namely, simple qualia, and insists that there are other individuals than simple qualia, namely, sums, we ask what more content a sum contains than the simple qualia in it.[27]

---

[25] This well may be Goodman's view. See his "The Way the World Is," *The Review of Metaphysics*, vol. 14 (1960), pp. 48–56.

[26] The former follows from the definition of the sum function, the latter is *SA* theorem 7.15, p. 176 (223).

[27] *Ibid.*, p. 86 (118). Goodman says: ". . . every admitted value of the individual variables of a finite system is a sum of, and in this sense reducible to, one or more atoms of the system." The sense of "reducible" is far from clear. If a sum contains no more content than its atoms—an atom is an individual with no systemic parts other than itself—then sums, like classes, seem to be mere fictions. Rather obviously, however, Goodman treats sums in a way which makes it clear that they are not so 'reducible.' For the sum of two qualia a and b is not merely a and not merely b, but a *and* b. But what interpretation can be given to "and"? It is this difficulty, and not necessarily the strange consequence that two colors or two places have a sum, which makes sums every bit as mysterious as classes. For an interesting discussion of the notion of addition of individuals see Russell's *The Principles of Mathematics* (2nd ed. New York; W. W. Norton & Co., 1938), p. 71.

Ohio State University

VI

Truth: Austin, Strawson, Warnock

TED HONDERICH

I

To say a statement is true, said Austin in the beginning,[1] is partly to say something about meaning rules or conventions:

> *descriptive* conventions correlating the words (=sentences) with the *types* of situation, thing, event, etc., to be found in the world,
> *demonstrative* conventions correlating the words (=statements) with the *historic* situations, etc., to be found in the world.

To say a statement is true is to say this:

> the historic state of affairs to which it is correlated by the demonstrative conventions (the one to which it "refers") is of a type with which the sentence used in making it is correlated by the descriptive conventions.

One inevitable question upon whose answer a great deal hangs is about the so-called "things," "events," "situations," and "states of affairs." Elsewhere they are "facts" and "features." Mr. Strawson, in his original reply,[2] took what he now[3] regards as the wrong view of what might be called their extent. Take the statement that we are awake. What is it that is correlated by the so-called demonstrative conventions with the statement, *us* or *our being awake*? Strawson originally chose us. In general, he took the worldly terms of "demonstrative conventions" to be *items* picked out by way of identifying substantival expressions in the sentences used to make the statements. He took these terms not to be *circumstances* specified, for example, by way of the subjects and predicates of sentences. I shall use these two words, "item" and "circumstance," for the two candidates for the worldly term of "demonstrative conventions." Items are what are referred to, in some ordinary philosophical sense, by substantival expressions. A circumstance is related, somehow, to the whole sen-

---

[1] J. L. Austin, "Truth," *Proceedings of the Aristotelian Society*, supplementary vol. 24 (1950).

[2] P. F. Strawson, "Truth," *ibid.*, Reprinted, as is Austin's paper, in G. Pitcher (ed.) *Truth* (Englewood Cliffs, 1964).

[3] "Truth: A Reconsideration of Austin's Views," *The Philosophical Quarterly*, vol. 15, (1965).

tence used to make the statement. Both items and circumstances are in the world.[4]

Mainly as a consequence of taking Austin's account to be about items, Strawson argued that even if it was correct as far as it went, it didn't go very far. It seemed to be an account of the truth of only affirmative categorical statements in which items are referred to in the familiar way. It thus appeared to be all too narrow. It did not seem to explain the truth of existential, general, or negative statements. It did not seem to explain in any plain way the truth of hypothetical or disjunctive statements. He now accepts, at Mr. Warnock's urging,[5] that Austin had in mind circumstances and not items as the worldly terms of his demonstrative conventions. To get distinct the two interpretations of the definition of truth, consider the statement made on some occasion in the words "That man looks puzzled." On the old interpretation of Austin's view, to say the statement is true is to say this:

> The item (a certain man) to which the statement is correlated by demonstrative conventions is of a type of item (those looking puzzled) with which the sentence used in making the statement is correlated by descriptive conventions.

On the new interpretation it is to say this:

> The circumstance (a certain man's looking puzzled) to which the statement is correlated by demonstrative conventions is of a type of circumstance (those of *a* or *some* man's looking puzzled) with which the sentence used to make the statement is correlated by descriptive conventions.

What can be said of the definition under the new interpretation? The first of Strawson's new criticisms[6] proceeds from consideration of a number of examples, of which one is: "That guest drank no wine at dinner." This sentence (not statement) is supposed to be correlated by "descriptive conventions" with a type of circumstance, the type of which all cases of *a or some guest's drinking no wine at dinner* are instances. Given this, Strawson says, it seems unquestionable that the "descriptive conventions" in question include at least those conventions which fix the meanings of the words "guest," "drink," "no," "wine," and "dinner." Suppose now that a statement is made by a use of the sentence "That guest drank no wine at dinner." We must note first that the "demonstrative conventions" involved in the making of any statement have come to be regarded as correlating a particular

---

[4] See Austin, "Unfair to Facts," *Philosophical Papers* (Oxford, 1961).

[5] G. J. Warnock, "Truth and Correspondence" in C. D. Rollins (ed.), *Knowledge and Experience* (Pittsburgh, 1962).

[6] In "Truth: A Reconsideration of Austin's Views," *op. cit.*

circumstance in the world *not* with the statement itself, but with the utterance of the sentence.[7] This is an amendment to Austin's original conception of demonstrative conventions, given in the passage quoted. The argument for the amendment is partly that the relation between a statement[8] and a particular circumstance is not one of convention, but rather a quite different relation of which I shall have something to say in a moment. That there *is* a conventional connection of some kind between the particular circumstance and something else is beyond question, and so the utterance is nominated. It also has claims of its own to the role. To return to the point, what are the "demonstrative conventions" involved in the making of a particular statement by a use of "That guest drank no wine at dinner"? It would be most unplausible, Strawson says, to think that the conventional meanings of the words "guest," "drank," "no," "wine," and "dinner," while clearly involved in correlating the sentence with a *type* of circumstance, are not involved in determining the reference of any particular utterance of the sentence.

If this is so, then one and the same convention may enter into both the correlation between utterance and circumstance and the correlation between sentence and type of circumstance. However, we have been talking as if there exist, with respect to a particular sentence and its uses, two quite independent groups of conventions. What we need is an amended formulation, which, as Strawson says, allows for any degree of overlap, up to identity, between the conventions involved in correlating utterances with circumstances and the conventions involved in uttering sentences with types of circumstances. We get something like this:

A statement is true when the circumstance with which the words used in making it are, as then used, correlated by semantic conventions, is of the type with which those words are standardly correlated by semantic conventions.

I agree that it is obviously mistaken to imply that there are independent sets of conventions when we take Austin's view to be about circumstances rather than items. It is obvious too, however, that substantially the same definition of truth persists in the new formulation just given, as Strawson accepts. I shall continue to talk of *demonstrative conventions* and *descriptive conventions*, but these labels

[7] Warnock, "A Problem About Truth" in George Pitcher (ed.), *op. cit.*

[8] Statements, as I understand them, may be identified crudely but serviceably by the specification that two utterances are of the same statement if they say the same thing about the same thing. See E. J. Lemmon, "Sentences, Statements and Propositions" in Bernard Williams and Alan Montefiore, *British Analytical Philosophy* (London, 1966).

will be restricted in use. By a demonstrative convention I shall mean only one that is functioning as part of the correlation between an utterance and a circumstance or item and not imply that the same convention might not correlate sentence and type of circumstance or item.

It is Strawson's second criticism, on which the remainder of his paper depends, that I wish to look at more closely: for the same sentence to be used on two occasions or by two persons to make the same statement. Austin said, with the usual ambiguity, the utterances must have reference to the same "situation or event." Take the sentence "The canal is deep with mud." What Austin very likely intended, and anyway what is true, is that it may be used on different occasions or by different persons to make the same statement if it is being used about the same canal. It may be so used, that is, if it has reference to the same *item* rather than *circumstance*. It is not necessary that the canal actually be deep with mud. There need not obtain or exist such a circumstance. For the sentence to be used by two people to make the same statement, they need not be talking about the same circumstance. If the canal isn't deep with mud, there will be no such circumstance.

On the basis of Austin's comment, or partly so, Warnock has attributed to him the view that "a statement is identified, in part, by reference to the situation to which it relates. What "demonstrative conventions" in part determine is . . . what statement is made by the utterance of certain words on a particular occasion."[9] That is, I take it, when I hear being uttered the words "The canal is deep with mud," I discover which of a number of possible statements is being made by discovering to which canal the utterance relates.

Now for Strawson's argument, of which I shall quote the first and fundamental part.

> The second deficiency [of Austin's account of truth] is revealed if one asks how exactly the particular historical situation in question in any case is to be specified. The Austin-Warnock view is that one does not know exactly what statement is being made in any case unless one knows what particular historical situation is being referred to. So presumably it must be possible in principle in every case to specify this situation. Now one might think at first that there was no particular difficulty about that. For suppose our statement is: "This inkwell has no ink in it." Then one might think that the particular historical situation in question is simply the situation of this particular inkwell's being inkless at the time at which the statement is made. And this is obviously a generalizable style of answer. But this style of answer won't do at all. For we are trying to

---

[9] "A Problem About Truth," *op. cit.*, p. 67.

specify the particular historical situation which it is a matter of the statement's *identity* that it refers to, and we must be able to do this in such a way as not to settle in advance the question of the statement's truth value and, moreover, settle it in favour of the statement's truth. If the historical situation which it is a matter of the statement's identity that it refers to was specifiable only in a way which had the consequence that the statement was true, then every statement . . . would be true; which is absurd. So we must think again.[10]

Strawson tries to find other ways of specifying the situation such that it doesn't follow that the related statement is true. He encounters difficulties and eventually draws the conclusion, not that there is something fishy with the argument about statement-identity, but that we must give up our account of truth. What I should like to say first is that there is no reason for supposing that we "radically depart" from the structure of the given account of truth if, as he says, we abandon the notion of an identified existing situation *which it is a matter of that statement's identity that it refers to* and with respect to which the question arises as to whether it is or isn't of a certain type. Certainly we radically depart if we abandon the notion of an existing situation which may or may not be of a certain type. But there is no good reason, and none at all given, for thinking that we depart from the given account if we say nothing at all about the conditions of identifying statements. We may be expected, of course, to specify the relation between statement and situation with respect to any true statement. Originally it was said simply that the statement itself is correlated with the situation by demonstrative conventions. Now we understand that this correlation holds between utterance and situation. The statement is related to the situation, we may now say, in that it is made by an utterance correlated by certain conventions with the situation. This by itself commits us to no specific view about the identity of statements.

Needless to say, the account of truth must be consistent with any true account of the identification of statements. Further, the two accounts together must not generate absurdities, such as the absurdity that all identifiable statements are true. What I should like to show now is that the only arguable account of statement identification in the field raises no difficulties for the account of truth. In formulating plainly the argument of quoted passage, incidentally, I intend no conjecture about what Warnock may have meant when he said in passing that "a statement is identified, in part, by reference to the situation to which it relates." I shall discuss only this: For a person to know what statement is being made on any occasion he must know the

---

[10] "Truth: A Reconsideration of Austin's Views," *op. cit.*, p. 295.

I

utterance to refer to some situation, some actual part of parts of the world; therefore the statement must be true.

Why, exactly, must there be a situation to which I know an utterance to refer if I am to identify the statement? If there is such a situation, must the statement be true? There are large and irritating questions in the wings, and indeed onstage, but I shall not pay them much attention. We know that to talk of *situations* in this context is ambiguous between talk of *items* and talk of *circumstances*. I suggest that the only possible argument leading to Strawson's conclusion gains what plausibility it has from this ambiguity. If we get rid of the ambiguity, no plausibility remains.

The argument, if we do not put in a premiss for every possible objection, may be put into three steps.

(1) Any statement, if it is to be identifiable, must refer.

(2) If it refers, there is a situation to which it refers.

(3) Given this situation, the statement is true.

Each of these claims, perhaps surprisingly, is true or at least arguable given one or the other of the two possible readings for "situation." The argument fails if we adopt either reading. I should like to show this both for its own sake and also because doing so will make clearer at least one important aspect of Austin's account of truth under the two interpretations. We first take the argument as being concerned with items, not circumstances.

(1) Any statement, if identifiable, must refer.

(2) If the statement refers, there is an *item* to which it refers.

What must be kept in mind here is something I have so far only implied, that the sense of talk about "referring" or "demonstrative conventions" varies systematically in this discussion according to what worldly term is understood. With a particular statement, different or rather *more* conventions enter into the correlations with a circumstance than with an item. (We are presently taking the worldly term to be an item.) Given this, part (1) of the argument is certainly false. It is false that all identifiable statements refer, in the sense in which there can be referring to items. Some statements, of course, do refer in this sense, which is the ordinary sense. What about (2)? This is for a number of reasons a quite discussable proposition, but one which I shall not discuss. Let us simply take the view of it favorable to the argument, that it is true, and pass on to

(3) Given this item, the statement is true.

Obviously this is false. Even if we confine ourselves to statements which do refer in the given ordinary sense, as we cannot, and if we grant that there must be items to which they refer, it cannot follow that the statements must be true. The truth of the statement that the canal is deep with mud doesn't follow from the existence of the canal. So much for the argument when construed as being about items.

Putting "circumstance" for "situation" in the argument, we get:

(1) Any statement, if identifiable, must refer.
(2) If a statement refers, there exists or obtains a circumstance to which it refers.

It is under this interpretation of the argument that one should be most cautious in talking of a statement referring or involving demonstrative conventions. With respect to such a statement as that the cat is on the mat, the related circumstance is specified by way of the subject and the predicate. To say that the statement refers to a circumstance, in the relevant sense, will be to say that it picks out an item and describes it. That is, to say here that a statement refers or is correlated by demonstrative conventions with a circumstance is to say that it refers and describes *in the ordinary senses*.

Given all this, is it true that any identifiable statement, which is to say any statement, must refer? This amounts to the question of whether any statement must pick out an item and describe it, as in the case just mentioned, or function in some other claim-making way. The answer, necessarily, is yes. But if (1) is true, the same is not the case with (2). To take the central cases, it does not follow from the facts that a statement refers and describes, in the ordinary senses, that there *is* a circumstance. A statement may describe without it being the case that there exists the relevant circumstance. There remains of the argument only

(5) Given that this circumstance obtains, the statement is true.

The circumstance does not obtain, necessarily, and so we need not worry about this conclusion. If the circumstance necessarily did obtain or exist, however, as is not the case with items, the statement would have to be true.

In summary: The claim that to know what statement is being made on some occasion I must know of a situation to which the utterance refers is ambiguous. If one takes it to be about items, there *may* be some argument for it, but there is no question of a further consequence —the statement's necessarily being true. It one takes the claim to be about circumstances, there is no argument for it. If there were a conclusive argument, there would be the consequence that the statement be true necessarily. In addition to this, there is the question of whether the account of truth integrally involves or entails the falsehood that to identify a statement we must identify a circumstance. The answer is no.

II

For all that has been said, I suggest, we may accept this account of truth, one got by understanding Austin's original account as mentioning circumstances. Is there anything else to be said against it? Let us first consider what is presented as its strength or anyway the absence of a defect. As we know, Strawson originally took Austin's account to be about items. He understood him, when he wrote of referring and of demonstrative conventions, to be thinking of "reference to particular objects or events made by means of definitely identifying substantival expressions occurring in the sentence uttered."[11] Given this understanding, as I have said, it seemed obvious to him that the given account of truth could at best explain, or explain satisfactorily, the truth of only a limited class of statements. These were affirmative categorical statements containing definitely identifying substantival expressions. It could not deal, or deal satisfactorily, with quite a number of other classes of statements: existential, general, negative, hypothetical, and disjunctive statements.

Warnock has argued that this defect, this narrowness, can be avoided by the shift from talk of items to talk of circumstances. He writes in one place:

> ... Austin's "purified version" of the Correspondence Theory is not, in my submission, grossly and intolerably restricted in its range of application in the way that Mr Strawson has suggested—restricted, that is, roughly speaking to the special case of subject-predicate statements about individual things. The restriction actually implied by ... incorporation into his account of truth of *both* demonstrative *and* descriptive conventions is, rather, that his account fits the case only of utterances which, in principle at least, we could be in a position to pronounce to be true on empirical grounds. [12]

Strawson now seems to accept this, as I have remarked, and that he does is given [13] as the *raison d'être* of the second thoughts of his which we have been considering. I should like to suggest that the account of truth in question is as narrow when taken to be about circumstances as when taken to be about items. Or, if it is to be described as narrow at all, it is as narrow under one interpretation as the other.

The existential statement that there are white cats, like any existential statement, does not involve referring in the ordinary sense. As Warnock rightly says, if I make the statement I do not allude to any

---

[11] *Ibid.*, p. 290.

[12] "Truth and Correspondence," *op. cit.*, p. 17. To suggest of the account that it should also cover necessary truth, as Warnock does, seems a touch demanding.

[13] "Truth: A Reconsideration of Austin's Views," *op. cit.*, pp. 290, 300.

white cats in particular and I cannot properly be asked *which* white cats I am saying that there are. And so, of course, one cannot explain straightforwardly how this statement can be true if one's account of truth requires of true statements that they refer in the ordinary sense. Warnock [14] seems confident that he can deal with existential statements on the revised account. It will be useful to state it again, first by way of an ordinary subject-predicate statement. Take the one made on some occasion in the words "That telephone is ringing." To say this is true, on the revised account, is to say that the circumstance to which it relates is of the type appropriate to the sentence, the type whose instances are cases of *some* or *a* telephone's ringing. More generally, to say any statement is true is to say a circumstance is of a type, the type related to the sentence. Let us now consider the existential statement that there are white cats. Can we explain its truth in any such way? It is clear that we can't. What circumstance would such an explanation mention? Presumably, as Warnock would say, there being white cats. But given this circumstance, of what possible type could it be an instance? From the sentence "That telephone is ringing" we could, by dropping some of the ordinary demonstrative conventions, move to a notion of the type all of whose instances are cases of some telephone's ringing. We can do no comparable thing with "There are white cats." There is no conceivable type which stands to the circumstance of *there being white cats* as *any telephone's ringing* stands to *a particular telephone's ringing*. In short, our account cannot explain the truth of existential statements straightforwardly.

To return momentarily to the old interpretation of Austin's view, it seems likely that one can give some account, if not a "straightforward" one, of the truth of existential statements. This will proceed by way of an analysis of existential statements which relates them to ordinary referring statements, whose truth *can* be explained by way of the primary definition. We might say, roughly, that to say the statement that there are white cats is true is to say that a referring statement in the words "That is a white cat" is sometimes true—in the primary sense. This leaves us with a different account of the truth of existential statements. All this seems obvious, and it also seems obvious that one can follow the same path if one takes the new interpretation of Austin's view. One can, that is, give an account of the truth of existential statements which turns on the account of the truth of more ordinary statements.

The new view and the old view, then, are exactly on a level with

[14] "Truth and Correspondence," *op. cit.*, pp. 15–16.

I*

respect to explaining the truth of existential statements. The same thing may be shown with general statements. Some such point, however, seems to be accepted by both Warnock and Strawson. What of the other sorts of recalcitrant statements? Given the account of truth in terms of items, negative statements were thought to present difficulty. Take the statement made by the words "He isn't in the library." In such a case, the difficulty was thought to be of a different kind, since ordinary negative statements may involve referring in the ordinary way. The difficulty was thought to have to do with specifying the type of item in question. Could one really talk of the type whose instances are cases of *not being in the library*? It was thought not, for no very clear reason. One could, of course, make another move. One could take the truth of our negative statement to consist in the fact that a certain item was *not* of a type correlated with *the affirmative form* of the statement. As in the case of existential and general statements this could be said to destroy the "simplicity" of the account of truth by introducing a new sense, strictly speaking, of "is true." What I wish to suggest is that the same difficulty arises for the account when it is taken to be about circumstances. Indeed, it arises over both the circumstance and the type of circumstance. Of course one can respond to difficulty in the same way as before.

There remain disjunctive and hypothetical statements. It was supposed that the old account faced difficulties in accounting for the truth of these. But what is the trouble with disjunctives? Take the statement that he is English or Greek. Why not say that for it to be true is for the item in question to be of the type whose instances are either English or Greek? There seems no good reason for thinking, certainly, that the account of truth could be applied only to particular disjuncts. Certainly if there are difficulties, they arise in a similar way on the revised definition. Hypotheticals are notoriously more difficult and I shall say only that a shift from circumstances is not going to make things easier.

III

The old and the new versions of Austin's view, then, appear to be about equally able to account for the truth of these different kinds of statement. Whether or not either version should be regarded as wanting because it does not provide what might be called a univocal account of the truth of diverse kinds of statements is something that seems not well established.[15] I shall say something more of the dis-

[15] Austin himself appears not to have been troubled. See n. 11, p. 23, "*Truth*," *op. cit.*

tinction between the two versions but I should like first to comment on another of Strawson's objections which might be thought critical for either. He implies in his recent paper that it is. The objection, first stated in his original paper, is that Austin's answer is not an answer to the question about truth which he took himself to be answering. That question is, according to Strawson, "How do we use the word 'true'?" or "What do we assert when we assert a statement to be true?" This question is to be sharply distinguished from what is called the problem of elucidating "fact-stating discourse." The question here may be put as "How do we state facts?" or "Under what semantic conditions do we make true statements?" It was allowed that in his account Austin had given an answer, although an inadequate one, to this second question. The correct answer to the first question, according to Strawson, is that in asserting a statement to be true we are asserting that statement and also performing a speech-act, one of agreeing, granting, corroborating, conceding, or whatever.

Warnock has made two replies to this.[16] The most effective begins from the fact that we do have in language a number of terms other than "is true" for signifying agreement and the rest, including "I agree," and "You're right." However, it is claimed, while we use most or all of them, including "is true," to indicate agreement after a statement has been made, we use "is true" *only* after statements. The others may turn up after, for example, recommendations and announcements of decisions. Given this, we are told, it is natural to think that "is true" not only expresses agreement or whatever, but also asserts something about the statement in question: what Austin says it asserts. This is something less than conclusive. It is not beyond question that "is true" turns up relevantly only in conjunction with statements. If it mainly does, this may be because it is in place when certain semantic conditions are satisfied. It still might not be that statements including "is true" assert that those conditions obtain. Nevertheless, if Warnock's reply is not conclusive, it might be held to have some force, or to reinforce what seems a likelihood, if the reasons for the opposing point of view are not coercive. One of them is the supposed correctness of Strawson's own answer to the first question, which I have mentioned and must here pass over. I wish merely to point out that the most explicit of Strawson's arguments against Austin leaves a great deal to be desired. In it, he appears to argue that Austin's answer is an answer to the wrong question by the procedure of misdescribing the answer. He writes in one place:

[16] "A Problem About Truth," *op. cit.*

If Mr. Austin is right in suggesting that to say that a statement is true is to say that "the historic state of affairs to which it . . . is correlated by the demonstrative conventions . . . is of a type with which the sentence used in making the statement is correlated by the descriptive conventions," *then* . . . in declaring a statement to be true we are either:

(a) talking about the meanings of the words used by the speaker whose making of the statement is the occasion for our use of "true" . . . or

(b) saying that the speaker has used correctly the words he did use.

It is *patently* false that we are doing either of these things.[17]

It does seem patently false that in declaring a statement to be true we are doing or only doing either of these vaguely-described things. It also seems false that this is the claim that we have been considering. In declaring a statement to be true we certainly are declaring something about a part of the world. The claim we have been considering includes this. What part, and what is said of it, is of course explained in terms of conventions which fix the meanings of words.

I conclude, then, that there seems little reason here to accept the unlikely view that the account we have been considering is not an answer to the question of what we assert when we assert a statement to be true.

IV

Finally, what is there to choose between the old and the new versions of Austin's definition? One consequence of the discussion in Sect. II is that one can have an idea of a relevant type of circumstance at all only for statements which involve referring in the ordinary sense. One describes a type related to a statement by eliminating references to a particular instance. The revised definition of truth, then, like the original one, applies directly only to statements involving ordinary referring. There is, of course, a remaining difference between the revised and original views. Take a statement made in the words "That clerk is very perceptive," where the man is not a clerk but is very perceptive. On the old view the statement is true, since the item in question is of a certain type, that one whose instances are very perceptive persons. On the new view it is false, since the circumstance is not one of some or a clerk's being very perceptive.

To say a statement is true on the new view, if we do some drastic pruning and take into account the initial limitation to one class of statements, is to say this: the circumstance referred to is as it is described to be. To talk of referring in this sense, as I have explained, is

---

[17] "Truth" in *Truth*, *op. cit.*, pp. 43–44.

to talk of the conventions linking both the subject and the predicate of the utterance with the world. We can then put the view more clearly as this: *To say a statement is true is to say that the item referred to and described, in the ordinary senses, is as referred to and described.* The old view, if we cast it in a similar form, is this: *To say a statement is true is to say in the ordinary senses that the item referred to is as described.* Deciding between the two views, which raises difficulties of a familiar nature, is something else that I shall not presently attempt. It might be taken to be a problem of a secondary nature when considered within the context of the present controversy about truth. Austin's view in either version, raises earlier questions. Those of them that have been considered in this paper seem open to answers. This may not be surprising given that the proposition put forward is so close to the truism that to say a statement is true is to say that things are as they are said to be.

University College, London

VII

Propositions and Abstract Propositions

COLWYN WILLIAMSON*

I. PROPOSITIONS AND SENTENCES

> ... they see in the essence, not something that already
> lies open to view and that becomes surveyable by a re-
> arrangement, but something that lies *beneath* the
> surface.
>
> *Ludwig Wittgenstein*

T HE proposition is not a sentence. Certainly the proposition is
intimately related to the sentence: an indicative sentence may
"express," "represent," "signify," "designate," or even "name"
a proposition; and a proposition may be the "intension," the "content," the "meaning," the "real meaning," or the "literal meaning"
of an indicative sentence. But a proposition is not the same as a
sentence, and to conflate the two is to render inexplicable several
commonplace phenomena, create an unworkable logic, generate an
uneconomical number of entities, make nonsense of mathematics,
make communication incomprehensible, and, in general, to cause
chaos and confusion where clarity could have reigned. These are the
more or less extravagent claims that may be made on behalf of the
viewpoint I shall call *abstractism*.

According to abstractism, the proposition is not on a par with the
sentence; it is not a certain kind of sentence; it is not a sentence looked
at from a particular angle. The proposition is not just a different
entity; it is a different kind of entity; it has a different order of being.
To speak of propositions in the way in which we speak of sentences is
to make a fundamental category mistake.[1] It is therefore necessary,
Church suggests, to make a distinction between proposition in the
"traditional" or "scholastic-traditional" sense, and proposition in

---

* Whatever thoughts I have had on these problems have been greatly stimulated
by arguments and discussions with Miss G. E. M. Anscombe and Professor A. J.
Ayer.

[1] R. D. Bradley, "Must the Future be What it is Going to Be?" *Mind*, vol. 68
(1959), uses a strong version of the sentence/proposition distinction in order,
allegedly, to solve the problem of logical determinism and fatalism.

138

the "abstract" sense. "A proposition in the abstract sense, unlike the traditional proposition, may not be said to be of any language; it is not a form of words, and it is not a linguistic entity of any kind except in the sense that it may be obtained by abstraction from language."[2] What are the initial impulses which give rise to this radical distinction between sentence and nonlinguistic proposition? The purpose of what follows immediately is briefly to outline and evaluate a standard elementary argument for the abstractist position.

The recipe for abstract propositions often goes as follows. Take an English declarative sentence, its translation into Latin, and its translation into French.[3] In the traditional sense, these are three different propositions. But this makes, for instance, the business of inference intolerably cumbrous. Every conjunction, disjunction, implication involving "Je pense donc je suis" would have no bearing on similar constructions involving "I think therefore I am" or "Cogito ergo sum." The proposition must, therefore, be something distinct from the sentence; or, at least, it would be inconvenient and uneconomical to identify propositions and sentences.

The abstract proposition is economical, then, in the sense that it cuts down the number of entities in the above case to one. Three sentences mean the same thing, and the same thing they all mean is an abstract proposition. The relation between sentence and abstract proposition has most frequently been called "meaning," and in some instances propositions are actually *defined* as the meaning of indicative sentences.[4]

An argument similar to the one outlined may be based on the fact that within a single language different sentences may have the same meaning. Once again, economy may be introduced by substituting for the many sentential-variations a single abstract proposition.

Some preliminary remarks about the argument so far: Nothing about the existence, or need for, an abstract, non-linguistic entity follows from the fact that different sentences—whether within a single or several different languages—can mean the same thing. There is little point in re-hashing the flaws in arguments which rely upon

[2] Alonzo Church, "Propositions and Sentences" in *The Problem of Universals: A Symposium*, by I. M. Bochenski, N. Goodman, and A. Church (Notre Dame 1956), p. 4. His view, Church says, is shared by Bolzano, Frege, Eaton, Cohen and Nagel, Lewis and Langford, Carnap, and the early Russell.

[3] Church, *op. cit.*

[4] See A. Ambrose and M. Lazerowitz, *Fundamentals of Symbolic Logic* (New York, 1948), p. 14; A. Pap, "Propositions, Sentences and the Semantic Definition of Truth," *Theoria*, vol. 22 (1954), p. 26 n; E. S. Brightman, *An Introduction to Philosophy* (3rd ed., revised by R. N. Beck; New York, 1964), p. 373.

expressions like "means something" and "mean the same thing." To say that an expression means something is not to say that it means some thing. And to deny that different sentences *point to* (as I shall say) an abstract proposition is not to deny that different sentences may mean the same thing. We must not let our forms of expression send us "in pursuit of chimeras."[5]

Church tells us[6] that someone who uses the abstract notion "has in mind the meaning rather than the meaning plus the words," and that "the content of meaning is what is common to the sentences in different languages." The meaning, Church says, is the "common property" of different sentences. But how are we to have in mind the meaning rather than the meaning plus words? Church implies that it may be done by taking the "composite entity, sentence plus (abstract) proposition" and subtracting, abstracting the "sentence as a syntactical entity, taken apart from its meaning." What remains will be an abstract proposition. All of this is very straightforward. For Church, we might say, the problem is mainly morphological: we used to call "apple" everything that came away from the bough when we plucked the fruit; now we use "apple" for the fruit with its stalk removed.

But is it so easy to pluck the meaning from the sentence?[7] There are, to be sure, situations in which I may know that a particular set of words make up a sentence, and yet not know what the sentence means. But this won't do, because, in order to obtain the abstract proposition, we have to arrive at the meaning minus the sentence, not the sentence minus its meaning; and that task seems absurd. The difficulty we find in assigning a practical significance to Church's proposed separation of sentence and meaning is not accidental so far as his whole enterprise is concerned. For, in asking us to think of sentences as syntactical entities, taken apart from their meaning, Church is creating a void in our language where "sentence" used to be. And it is just because "sentence" is not, typically, the same as "sentence treated as a pure syntactical entity" that we suddenly feel a need for Church's use of "proposition": "proposition" is now doing what "sentence" used to do perfectly well.

In both the argument from different languages and the argument from a single language, it is claimed that the introduction of abstract

[5] L. Wittgenstein, *Philosophical Investigations*, §94.
[6] *Op. cit.*, pp. 4–6.
[7] G. E. Moore also examined the problem of splitting the composite entity, sentence plus meaning, and came to the conclusion that the two parts of the entity fall under "two acts of consciousness." *Some Main Problems of Philosophy* (London and New York, 1953), p. 57.

propositions secures an economy of entities. Unfortunately, there are two ways of looking at the proposed economy. We may see it as replacing a number of entities (sentences which mean the same thing) with one entity (the proposition they all point to); but we may also see it as adding one more entity to the existing list. Of course, such a controversy would be completely pointless (though, for all that, it would be remarkably like a number of philosophical arguments[8]), but it does lead us to ask: what is *practical* significance of the supposed economy? The economy claimed seems somewhat unhelpful when we reconcile ourselves to the fact that philosophers and logicians must themselves speak in English, Polish, or whatever. The consolation that a philosopher derives from the knowledge that he and philosophers of other nationalities are pointing to the same abstract proposition is itself abstract; for he still has to make do with a sentence to point to that proposition. It is all very well to claim that "the proposition of which a sentence is the verbal expression is distinct from the visual marks or sound waves of the expression." But this seems less than helpful when it is added that "it should be noted, however, that while the proposition must not be confused with the symbols that state it, no proposition can be *expressed* or *conveyed* without symbols."[9] The economy claimed for the abstract proposition is such that only a being capable of the *direct apprehension*, and use, of abstract propositions is able to take advantage of the reduction of entities. The economy is of no use to mortals, who have to rest content with signs, words, sentences, and the like. Which means: it is no use whatsoever.

II. Propositions and Propositional Variables

Ayer has claimed that we need propositions (in addition to sentences) in order to cover cases where we *refer to the proposition without specifying the sentence.*[10] Ayer writes: "it is necessary to have such a word in order that one may be able to refer to the meaning of sentences without having to specify them particularly." As an example, Ayer gives:

in the course of his speech he asserted a number of propositions of which I can now remember nothing except that at least three of them were false

---

[8] Thus, in the Great American Debate between "nominalists" and "realists" both sides claim, with equal right, to be in favor of economy.

[9] Morris Cohen and Ernest Nagel, *An Introduction to Logic and Scientific Method* (London, 1952), p. 27.

[10] A. J. Ayer, *The Foundations of Empirical Knowledge* (London, 1961), p. 101.

Why do we need to speak of propositions?

> The answer is that we often wish to make statements which apply not merely to a given indicative sentence, but also to any other sentence, whether of the same or of a different language, that has the same meaning; and our use of the word "proposition" enables us to do this concisely.[11]

Three separable points are raised by Ayer in the passages cited. The first has to do with "proposition" referring to the meaning of a sentence, not the sentence. The difficulties in this conception cannot be avoided by suggesting that it is merely terminological, a matter of definition, whether we use "proposition" for this or that.[12] The concept of proposition is tied, not only to sentences and meaning, but also to "true" and "false," "propositional logic," and so on. It will not do simply to say that the term is to be applied to the meaning of a sentence unless an account of meaning can be given which allows propositions to do the other jobs required of them. I do not believe that such an account can be given.

The second point has to do with the convenience gained by employing "proposition" in this way. There is nothing extraordinary about wanting to refer to a number of sentences, but Ayer is surely wrong to think that this consideration attaches special weight to any account of the nature of propositions. This may be confirmed by comparing Ayer's position with the view that he imagines to be the only real alternative, namely that a proposition is a sentence and the identity of a proposition is determined by the precise form of words involved. Imagine the following injunction: "and anything that is said, in the following pages, of a particular proposition may also be assumed to hold of any other proposition, in this or another language, always provided that the other proposition has the same meaning as the one mentioned." It is true that such an account would have many propositions where Ayer has one; but in terms of actual convenience is there any reason to reject it in favor of abstractism?

The third point has to do with the significance Ayer attaches to his example about remembering that a speech contained false propositions, but not remembering what those propositions were. Consider:

> in the course of his speech he asked a number of questions of which I can now remember nothing except that at least three of them were rhetorical.

Would Ayer claim that this shows the need to distinguish between, let us say, the sentence-question and the abstract question? Would he

[11] *Ibid.*, p. 102.
[12] See Carnap's "Empiricism, Semantics, and Ontology," *Revue Internationale de Philosophie*, vol. 4 (1950).

describe it as a case of referring to the abstract question without specifying the sentence-question? Well, perhaps he would. But although Ayer insists that his example must be described as "referring to propositions without specifying sentences," it could equally well be described as "referring to propositions without specifying *them*."[13] The inference that Ayer draws from his description of the example has already been written into that description. To say "there are some propositions such that he asserted them" is not to *refer to* any propositions. What Ayer's example actually shows is not the need for abstract propositions, but the need for *propositional variables*. Cases like "What the policeman said was true" prove nothing about the nature of propositions; they merely show the need for (or, more exactly, illustrate the role of) variables, or their ordinary language equivalents. We may, if we wish, call them "sentential variables"; or we may call them "propositional variables" and go on to give an account of propositions which identifies them, in one sense or another, with sentences.

Again and again we bump against the basic conviction (prejudice) that all examples illustrate the distinction between sentences and propositions. And behind this, in turn, is a vision according to which sentences come and go, but propositions go on forever. The exploration of the metaphysical significance of abstract propositions cannot be settled with a cheerful observation:

> is the proposition an objectionable metaphysical entity? The answer to this is: some of the reasons for introducing the notion of proposition, though humdrum, are good; therefore the notion so introduced is not an objectionable metaphysical entity.[14]

Of course, whether or not the notion of proposition should be "introduced" is not at stake, and could not be at stake unless the abstractist approach is presupposed. The question at issue is our *understanding* of the notion of proposition. And to see the abstract proposition as a metaphysical entity is not merely to demonstrate the flaws in a string of arguments (though that must be done), but also to comprehend the vision of an essence behind appearances, the attempt to find the ideal and separate it from the ordinary.

III. Propositions and the Objectivity of Truth

Truth is clearly independent. It has its own stubborn nature, to which our thinking must conform on pain of failure, i.e., error. We do not

---

[13] In this case, "referring to the *truth* of the propositions without specifying them" would seem to be even better.

[14] J. Teichmann, "Propositions," *The Philosophical Review*, vol. 70 (1961), p. 515.

make or alter truth by our thinking, any more than we make or alter goodness by our conduct, or beauty by our love or by our artistic endeavours. Truth is discovered, and not invented; and its nature is unaffected by the time and process of discovery, and careless of the personality of the discoverer. [15]

An argument in favor of the abstract proposition may be based on the Objectivity of Truth. [16] Propositions are true or false, and their truth or falsity is independent of whether I assert or deny them. That is, "thinking them is a case of discovering something," and a truth must "not vanish when one ceases to think of it." I may discover truths; I may fail to assert them; I may assert truths and subsequently forget them, and so on; but the truths exist independently of my activities. The proposition is what is true; what is true may go unasserted, i.e., never be expressed by a sentence; therefore, the proposition cannot be a sentence. What is true, the proposition, exists independently of my invention or construction of sentences. [17]

The argument from the Objectivity of Truth reflects a basic feeling about propositions, but it is not a good argument. "Truth" has a *substantive* and a *predicative* role. "His religion is based on seven great truths" (seven important true propositions, perhaps). But, "There was some truth in what he said." There is truth *of* a proposition, and the truth that *is* a proposition. If a proposition "has truth," it is "a truth." From the Objectivity of predicative truth (that a proposi-

---

[15] H. H. Joachim, *The Nature of Truth* (Oxford, 1906), p. 20.

[16] This title has been given to the argument by one who employs it, A. D. Woozley, *Theory of Knowledge: An Introduction* (London, 1949). The quotations in this paragraph are from p. 105.

[17] In connection with "truth is discovered, not invented," see the argument advanced by Church (*op. cit.*, pp. 8–9) in favor of abstract propositions on the basis of: "the distinction between there being in principle no proof of a particular proposed mathematical theorem (for example the Godel undecidable sentence) and there being no proof of it actually written out because all are too long." In other words: if a proposition is a sentence, then a proof is a series of sentences. Thus, when there is no series of sentences (because the writing would take too long), there is no proof. But there are two senses of "there being a proof" and "knowing there is no proof." There may be no proof ("in principle") because we have constructed a series of sentences which show that, according to our rules of construction, a particular further series of sentences cannot be constructed; and there may also be no proof in the sense that a particular series of sentences has not, or not yet, been constructed. Correspondingly, there are two cases in which we know that there is a proof. We can know that there is a proof of a particular theorem because we have constructed a series of sentences which constitute that proof: we can also know that there is a proof because we have constructed a series of sentences which shows that another series could be constructed, granted our rules for construction. The "could," then, refers to what is possible according to our procedural rules, not what is possible according to the amount of paper in the world or the length of a logician's life.

tion is true) nothing follows concerning the Objectivity of substantive truth (the true proposition). "Water boils at 100 degrees Centigrade, Normal Pressure." The Objectivity of Truth here could mean: you cannot alter the boiling point of water by asserting or denying that it boils at a certain temperature; and that, no doubt, is true. But there is language and the world of difference between a proposition and what makes it true. But "what makes the proposition true": is the meaning of that clear? What makes the proposition that water boils at 100 degress true? Water boils at 100 degress. We feel constrained, trapped in the proposition: "When we say, and *mean*, that such-and such is the case, we—and our meaning—do not stop anywhere short of the fact; but we mean: *this-is-so.*"[18] But the solution to these difficulties lies in our actual practice. How do we deal with someone who asks: what makes this true? We might go over a deduction, conduct or re-peat an experiment (with a Bunsen burner and a thermometer), recommend certain reading material, cite our experiences, and so on.[19] And we should always ask, when someone speaks of "what makes a proposition true," *which* proposition? Some of our difficulties spring from never seeing propositions, but only *the* proposition.

Suppose the abstractist says: any theory of propositions must accommodate the possibility of *real disagreement*.[20] Facts are not incompatible with one another: the claim that somethings is incom-patible with a fact is the same as the claim that something is not a fact. And no sentence, in itself, is incompatible with any other sentence. "This apple is red" and "This apple is not red" can be fitted into contexts such that these sentences are not incompatible. Hence, for there to be real disagreement is for propositions to be distinct from both facts and sentences. The simple reply to this (and, since we will

[18] Wittgenstein, *op. cit.*, §95. Cf. J. L. Austin, "Truth," *Proceedings of the Aristotelian Society*, Supplementary Volume 24, (1950), pp. 117–118. "When a statement is true, there is, *of course*, a state of affairs which makes it true and which is *toto mundo* distinct from the true statement about it: but equally of course, we can only *describe* that state of affairs *in words* (either the same or, with luck, others)."

[19] As a matter of fact, though, the only item on this list which corresponds at all commonly to "What makes this true?" is going over a deduction, or some informal equivalent. As far as the others are concerned, questions like "Why do you say this?" would more naturally be used. It is rather that the list corresponds to what the philosopher *ought* to have in mind when he speaks, at this level of generality, of "what makes the proposition true." This point should also affect our evaluation of what Austin says (see n. 18).

[20] This argument is based on that advanced by Woozley, *op. cit.*, p. 109. For an account of this and the previous argument from Objectivity cf. Gilbert Ryle, "Are there Propositions?" *Proceedings of the Aristotelian Society*, vol. 30 (1929–30), pp. 98–99. For Strawson's variation on the incompatibility argument see the following section.

explore part of this argument more fully in Sect. IV, it will do for the moment) is that pairs of propositions which we can imagine in contexts such that they would not be incompatible can also be imagined in contexts where they would be incompatible. If contexts show the absence of incompatibility, they can also show its presence. We are misled by our ability to conceive of sentences "in themselves," or as "syntactical" entities, into thinking that this is *all* there is to them. And so it is—just as all there is to an axe is wood and metal. The claim that an axe is not just metal and wood can mean either that it also contains a nail, or that an axe is a fairly specialized tool. Someone who says that human beings are not just collections of cells might mean that the body contains non-cellular tissue; he might also mean that we should not underestimate the moral and creative capacities of men. If we are inclined to think that a proposition is not just a sentence, this need not send us in search of some further object.[21] (And the abstract entity is a sign, not that the problem has been solved, but that it has been given up in despair.)

IV. Sentences and Statements

The claim that no sentence is incompatible with another, which provides Woozley with the basis for his distinction between sentence and proposition, also inspires Strawson's distinction between sentence and *statement*:

> I have spoken of *statements* as being inconsistent with each other; and there is a temptation to think that in this context we mean by a statement the same thing as a sentence of a certain kind; or, perhaps, the meaning of such a sentence. But suppose I write on the blackboard the following two pairs of sentences: (i) "I am under six foot tall" and "I am over six foot tall"; (ii) "The conductor is a bachelor" and "The conductor is married." In writing the sentences on the blackboard, I have, of course not contradicted myself; for I have written them there with a purely illustrative intention, in giving an English lesson.[22]

Suppose that I am conducting a class on Tool Design and that I hold up a piece of metal attached to a shaft of wood, and a metal rod attached to a wooden handle. My intention is purely illustrative: I want to make some point about the way in which tools are fashioned.

---

[21] "There seems to me to be no point in saying that there are no such things as propositions unless this means that there is no such thing as the thing that is said, over and above the sentence saying it. But this is manifestly false." (Teichmann, *op. cit.*, p. 501.) If Mrs. Teichmann does not intend "there is such a thing as the thing that is said" to be pleonastic, then it is (manifestly) false.

[22] P. F. Strawson, *Introduction to Logical Theory* (London, 1952), p. 3.

Does it follow that the object I hold up is not an axe? Or is it simply that I may use this object for a variety of purposes? That indicative sentences may be used in different ways does not imply that there is not a propositional use, i.e., a use such that, when the sentence is used in this way, we call it a proposition. It is not true that "What these examples show is that we cannot identify that which is true or false (the statement) with the sentence used in making it."[23] What actually follows is that we must not conflate the use of sentences to make statements with the use of sentences to refrain from making statements.[24] The problems concerning contradiction which move Strawson to press the sentence/statement distinction are not solved by the introduction of that distinction. For suppose that you make the *statement* that Jones is ill, and I make the *statement* that Jones is not ill. Have we contradicted one another? It is true that there is no necessity about "I am under six foot tall" and "I am over six foot tall" being inconsistent; but it is equally true that my *statements* to these effects need not be inconsistent. (And if it turns out that these are not yet, for Strawson, properly formed statements, then *this* is what he is about, and not the sentence/statement distinction.) Problems as to how propositions can be inconsistent are not caused by focussing our attention on the *wrong entity*, but by neglect of the *contexts* which make contradiction intelligible. Strawson is aware of the importance of context: "One thinks of both sentences as being uttered, in the same breath, by the same person."[25] But he does not seem to realize that this kind of explanation is perfectly adequate as it stands, and that the sentence/statement distinction adds nothing. What Strawson actually proves, and with this we should agree, is that we cannot identify "that which is true or false" with indicative sentences in contexts where no question as to truth or falsity could sensibly arise.

Strawson prefers "statements" to "propositions," probably for the good reason that the latter term has been tainted by Church's "modern times," and identified with the meaning of sentences. But, although many abstractists do identify propositions with meanings, and even more base their account on what it is for different sentences to "mean

[23] *Ibid.*, p. 4.
[24] Of course, "the use of sentences to refrain from making statements" is ambiguous between having as my intention refraining from making a statement, and having some intention which merely involves not making a statement (Strawson's example can be one or the other, depending how you look at it). What I have said applies to both cases.
[25] Strawson, *op. cit.* Of course, when trying to exemplify *contradiction* one thinks of both sentences being uttered in the same breath, by the same person. Otherwise, quite otherwise.

the same thing," the essence of abstractism does not lie in these specific conceptions, but in the conviction that the proposition must be some object distinct from the sentence: it is on this count that Strawson must be reckoned an abstractist.

"But doesn't Strawson distinguish between a sentence and a use of a sentence,[26] and isn't that rather like the sort of thing you want to say about propositions?" Strawson's position represents a version of abstractism purified by current preoccupations with "use." But the abstractist theory requires not purification, but elimination.

> ... we cannot talk of *the sentence* being true or false, but only of its being used to make a true or false assertion, or (if this is preferred) to express a true or false proposition. And equally obviously we cannot talk of *the sentence* being *about* a particular person, for the same sentence may be used at different times to talk about quite different particular persons, but only of *a use* of the sentence to talk about a particular person.[27]

But imagine someone who argued: since one and the same nail may be used on different occasions to join quite different pieces of wood, we cannot say that at any particular time it is joining *these* pieces. Now, in order to determine *which* particular person *this* sentence is about, we have to refer to what might be called *use*; but that is a different question.[28]

What, according to Strawson, is a proposition? Strawson himself rules out two possibilities—the sentence, and the meaning of the sentence. Perhaps the proposition is *a use* of a sentence? But that view is unintelligible. Although the *account* of "a use" could be true or false (contain true or false propositions!), "a use" itself cannot

[26] P. F. Strawson, "On Referring," *Mind*, vol. 59 (1950); reprinted in *Essays in Conceptual Analysis*, ed. A. Flew (London, 1956).

[27] *Ibid.*, pp. 28–29.

[28] Presumably Strawson would deny that the relation between sentence and statement is at all like that between a sentence and what it is *about*, but it is noteworthy that his argument gains some force from the juxtaposition of these relations. For it is only when we assume that a proposition is *particular* in something like the way in which a *person* is a particular person that the argument even gets started. And this *particularity* of the proposition, it would seem, has mainly to do with *reference* and *truth-value*. If we did not, in advance, assume this particularity, we would feel perfectly prepared to describe Strawson's data as: the same sentence (proposition, statement) may be used at different times and places to refer to different things, and so as to be now true, now false. But I will not deal with propositions and *tenses* at the moment; for even the nominalist opponents of abstractism (if they really are opponents) share this opposition to the notion of *tensed propositions*.

sensibly be described in this way.[29] We cannot substitute "uses" in our propositional calculi.

Strawson claims that "it is senseless to ask, of the *sentence*, whether it is true or false."[30] It would be extravagent to say that "This sentence is true" is senseless. On the other hand, "The sentence is true" and "The sentence is what is true or false" certainly do have a strange ring about them. But the strangeness is at the same time familiar: it is the strangeness of *philosophy*. The philosopher wishes to provide a *formal* answer to the question: What is true or false? When he asks this question, he is hunting for a *philosophical object:* propositions, sentences, statements, and assertions are such objects. It is for this reason that an appeal to our ordinary linguistic practices can somehow miss the point: the philosopher, because he asks "What is true?" in a very special way, cannot find a direct answer in the ordinary situations in which we ask and answer this question. Our ordinary practice might, in some sense or another, provide an *alternative* to philosophy (the study of it might, for example, wean us of the desire to find philosophical objects); but it cannot directly answer the philosophical question. Precisely because he cannot resist asking questions about the form of the universe, the philosopher cannot hope to find unambiguous answers in its actual content.

V. PROPOSITIONS

The purpose of what I have been doing is essentially negative: I have been trying to clear the way, do away with the philosophy. I should like to feel that it is *obvious* that a proposition is a sentence. A proposition is not "expressed," "denoted," or "meant" by a sentence: it *is* a sentence. A proposition is a sentence in the sense in which an axe is a piece of metal attached to a length of wood.[31] This is *all* there is to a proposition in the way in which this is all there is to an axe. And a proposition is *not just* a sentence in the way in which an axe is not just the metal and wood of which it is made.

But to establish the substance of the proposition is merely a preliminary to the real task, which is to attain some clarity about what it

[29] We can speak of something being put to its true (proper) use, but that is another kettle of fish.

[30] *Introduction to Logical Theory, op. cit.*, p. 175. For reasons consistent with the general purpose of this paper I have been unfair to Strawson by stressing only the abstractist strands in his thought. See n. 32.

[31] Teichmann, *op, cit.*, says, quite correctly, that a proposition is a sentence in the sense in which the king in chess is a piece of ivory. (A picture which we both owe to Miss Anscombe.) My suspicion, however, is that Mrs. Teichmann goes on to give an abstractist account of chess.

is that makes a sentence a proposition.[32] When we try to explain this, we tend at first to expect too much of the *symbols themselves*. We tell someone that such-and-such is a proposition, and he then observes this symbol being used in an English lesson in the way described by Strawson. And perhaps he concludes: That symbol couldn't have been a proposition! (Compare with: I tell someone that such-and-such is an axe, and later he observes it being used, upside down, as a hammer.) But this mistake stems from a one-sided vision of, as it were, the matter divorced from its motions:

> A glass is undoubtedly a glass cylinder and a drinking vessel. . . . A glass is a heavy object which may be used as a missile. A glass may serve as a paperweight, as a jar to keep a captive butterfly in, a glass may have value as an object with an artistic engraving or design, quite apart from the fact that it can be used as a drinking vessel, that it is made of glass, that its form is cylindrical, or not quite so, and so on and so forth.[33]

One final remark. Most abstractists, as we have seen, proceed as though we were already clear in our minds as to what an indicative (or declarative) sentence is, and therefore able to go on to the (separate) task of determining the nature of what is true or false, the proposition. But I do not believe that it is possible to give a purely, shall we say, "grammatical" definition of indicative or declarative sentences; and to describe what it is that makes a sentence indicative is already to describe the proposition. To imagine ourselves not knowing what propositions are is also to imagine ourselves unable to recognize indicative or declarative sentences.

"A proposition is a queer thing!"[34] That is true, but only if we allow it to be so. And the escape from abstractism lies in the realization that we should not seek an explanation of the peculiarities of our language in the multiplication of entities, but in language comprehended as human practice.

[32] It is on this question that it is possible to find common ground with some philosophers who might superficially seem to be opponents, because they reject the sentence in favor of assertions, statements, etc. In our terms, they are about the business of clarifying the context of practices which enable a sentence to be a proposition. See, for example, R. Cartwright, "Propositions," *Analytical Philosophy*, First Series, ed. R. Butler (Oxford, 1962). To some extent, the same should be said of Strawson.

[33] V. I. Lenin, *Selected Works*, vol. 9, ed. J. Fineberg (London, 1937), p. 65.

[34] "A proposition is a queer thing!" Here we have in germ the subliming of our whole account of logic. The tendency to assume a pure intermediary between the propositional *signs* and the facts, or even to try to purify, to sublime, the signs themselves. For our forms of expression prevent us in all sorts of ways from seeing that nothing out of the ordinary is involved, by sending us in pursuit of chimeras. See Wittgenstein, *Investigations*, §94.

University College of Swansea

Index of Names